SMALL

CHANGES,

BIG
IMPACT

10 Strategies to Promote Student Efficacy and Lifelong Learning

ANTHONY R. REIBEL
MATT THEDE

Solution Tree | Press

Copyright © 2020 by Solution Tree Press

Materials appearing here are copyrighted. With one exception, all rights are reserved. Readers may reproduce only those pages marked "Reproducible." Otherwise, no part of this book may be reproduced or transmitted in any form or by any means (electronic, photocopying, recording, or otherwise) without prior written permission of the publisher.

555 North Morton Street
Bloomington, IN 47404
800.733.6786 (toll free) / 812.336.7700
FAX: 812.336.7790

email: info@SolutionTree.com
SolutionTree.com

Visit **go.SolutionTree.com/schoolimprovement** to download the free reproducibles in this book.

Printed in the United States of America

Library of Congress Cataloging-in-Publication Data

Names: Reibel, Anthony R., author. | Thede, Matt, author.
Title: Small changes, big impact : ten strategies to promote student
  efficacy and lifelong learning / Anthony R. Reibel, Matt Thede.
Description: Bloomington, IN : Solution Tree Press, [2020] | Includes
  bibliographical references and index.
Identifiers: LCCN 2020000377 (print) | LCCN 2020000378 (ebook) | ISBN
  9781949539295 (paperback) | ISBN 9781949539301 (ebook)
Subjects: LCSH: School improvement programs--United States. | Academic
  achievement--United States. | Curriculum change--United States. |
  Effective teaching--United States. | Student-centered learning--United
  States. | Active learning--United States. | Educational
  evaluation--United States.
Classification: LCC LB2822.82 .R4 2020 (print) | LCC LB2822.82 (ebook) |
  DDC 371.2/07--dc23
LC record available at https://lccn.loc.gov/2020000377
LC ebook record available at https://lccn.loc.gov/2020000378

Solution Tree
Jeffrey C. Jones, CEO
Edmund M. Ackerman, President

Solution Tree Press
President and Publisher: Douglas M. Rife
Associate Publisher: Sarah Payne-Mills
Art Director: Rian Anderson
Managing Production Editor: Kendra Slayton
Senior Production Editor: Christine Hood
Content Development Specialist: Amy Rubenstein
Copy Editor: Kate St. Ives
Proofreader: Sarah Ludwig
Text and Cover Designer: Kelsey Hergül
Editorial Assistants: Sarah Ludwig and Elijah Oates

ACKNOWLEDGMENTS

As always, I want to thank my wife. Since the day we met, I continue to be in awe of her kindness, intelligence, and patience. Second, I would like to thank my mentors, Eric Twadell, Troy Gobble, and Mark Onuscheck. You have taught me more than you know about education, family, and life. And last, I want to thank the publisher, Solution Tree, for the continued support of these ideas and concepts.

—Anthony Reibel

I would like to thank my wife for the support she has shown me throughout our life together. As an educator herself, I am fortunate to be able to witness her amazing dedication and work for her students. In addition, I would like to thank some mentors in the field, Matt Townsley and Anthony Reibel, for always pushing my thinking and guiding me throughout my own personal journey. Finally, I would like to thank Steve Brand, Greg Batenhorst, and all our staff for their continued support in doing what is best for students.

—Matt Thede

Solution Tree Press would like to thank the following reviewers:

Kelly Grigsby
Academic Dean
Escondido High School
Escondido, California

Megan Grube
Director of Curriculum, Instruction, and Technology
Grand Isle Supervisory Union
Grand Isle, Vermont

Justin Holmquest
Principal
New Prairie Middle School
Carlisle, Indiana

Joshua Kunnath
English Teacher and
    Department Chair
Highland High School
Bakersfield, California

Faith Short
Assistant Principal
East Pointe Elementary School
Greenwood, Arkansas

Barry Thomas
Principal
Corunna High School
Corunna, Michigan

Steven Weber
Associate Superintendent for Teaching and Learning
Fayetteville Public Schools
Fayetteville, Arkansas

Erik Youngman
Director of Curriculum, Instruction, and Assessment
Libertyville District 70
Libertyville, Illinois

Visit **go.SolutionTree.com/schoolimprovement** to download the free reproducibles in this book.

TABLE OF CONTENTS

Reproducible pages are in italics.

About the Authors xi

Introduction 1
   About This Book 2
   A Final Thought 5

CHAPTER 1
Redefine Student Success 7
   What Student Success Looks Like 8
   Guidelines for Redefining Success 8
      Positive Self-Concept 9
      Self-Sustenance 9
      Accurate Perception of Abilities 10
      Social Connection and Emotional Awareness 11
      Articulation and Communication 11
   What Student Learning Looks Like 12
   Guidelines for Defining Learning 12
      Personal Agency 13
      Generative Learning 13
      Rooted Competence 13
      Constructive Failure 13
   Conclusion 14
   Big-Impact Recommendations for Implementation 14

CHAPTER 2
Create Student-Centered Mission Statements 15
   Characteristics of a Student-Centered Mission Statement 16
      Academic Acuity and Interest 16

    Social Connection. 16
    Emotional Awareness and Self-Concept. 17
    Self-Efficacy 17
How to Develop Student-Centered Mission Statements 18
    Values Self-Reliant Learning. 19
    Guards Against Transient Learning 19
    Doesn't Make Assumptions About Student Learning. 19
    Avoids Common Misperceptions About Student Learning. 20
    Uses Student-Produced Evidence to Make Decisions. 20
Conclusion. 21
Big-Impact Recommendations for Implementation 21

CHAPTER 3

Organize Curriculum Around Skills, Not Content 23

Create a Skills-Based Curricular Structure. 24
    Start With Enduring, Transferable Skills 24
    Create a Standard or Standards for Each Skill. 25
    Develop Proficiency Gradations for Each Standard 26
    Set Criteria for Each Proficiency Gradation 28
Know the Difference Between Proficiency Gradations and
    Learning Progressions. 31
Differentiate Between Recursive and Nonrecursive Criteria. 34
Conclusion. 36
Big-Impact Recommendations for Implementation 36
Course Description. 38

CHAPTER 4

Develop Student-Centered Rubrics 43

How to Create Student-Centered Rubrics. 44
How to Use Student-Centered Rubrics 49
    Student-Centered Rubrics Are for Conversation; Traditional Rubrics
        Are Primarily for Evaluation 49
    Student-Centered Rubrics Allow Students to Give Themselves
        Feedback; Traditional Rubrics Provide Feedback to Students 51
    Student-Centered Rubrics Appear Throughout the Learning Process;
        Traditional Rubrics Appear at the End of the Learning Process 52
Conclusion. 52
Big-Impact Recommendations for Implementation 53
Blank Rubric 54

Table of Contents

CHAPTER 5
Use Assessment as a Process for Learning ... 55
How to Create Process-Based Assessments ... 57
    Let Standards Guide Assessment Development ... 57
    View Assessments as Experiences, Not Events ... 58
    Use Assessments to Get to Know Students ... 58
    Implement Simulations, as They Are Crucial to Learning ... 59
    Make Sure Assessments Are Assumption Proof ... 59
Conclusion ... 61
Big-Impact Recommendations for Implementation ... 61
Planning Assessment and Instruction as a Continual Learning and Reflection Process ... *62*
Gathering the Right Evidence ... *63*

CHAPTER 6
Implement a Generative Learning Model of Instruction ... 65
Characteristics of a Generative Learning Model ... 65
How to Implement a Generative Model of Instruction ... 67
    Design Mastery Experiences, Not Lessons ... 67
    Align Instruction to the True Nature of Learning ... 69
    Use Proficiency Gradations During Instruction ... 70
    Leverage the Inseparability of Instruction and Assessment ... 71
    Use a Diamond Structure When Lesson Planning ... 73
    Teach With Student Thinking ... 75
Conclusion ... 75
Big-Impact Recommendations for Implementation ... 75
Planning Instruction Using Proficiency Gradations ... *77*
Instructional Diamond Template ... *78*

CHAPTER 7
Provide Critical, Growth-Based Feedback ... 79
How to Provide Critical, Growth-Based Feedback to Students ... 80
    Use Rubrics to Give Prescriptive Feedback, Not Diagnostic ... 80
    Use Summative Experiences Throughout a Unit ... 81
    Use Rubrics to Invite Students Into the Feedback Conversation ... 82
    Use Positive Language on Rubrics ... 83
    Be Positive, Not Punitive ... 83
    Use Nonevaluative Language Before Evaluative Language in Feedback ... 84
Conclusion ... 85

Big-Impact Recommendations for Implementation 85
　　Changing Diagnostic Feedback to Prescriptive Feedback 86
　　Success Criteria That Lends Itself to Co-Constructed Feedback 87

CHAPTER 8
Leverage Reflection and Reperformance 89
　　How to Add More Student Reflection to Lessons. 90
　　　　Serious Self-Questioning. 91
　　　　Self-Deliberation. 91
　　　　Reliable Reflective Mechanics. 92
　　　　Differentiated Reflection. 93
　　Reperformance 95
　　　　Reassessments in Practice 95
　　　　Reperformances in Practice. 96
　　Conclusion. 96
　　Big-Impact Recommendations for Implementation 97

CHAPTER 9
Use Evidence-Based Grading Practices 99
　　How to Use Evidence for Determining Grades 100
　　　　Inform Professional Judgment With Evidence 100
　　　　Align Proficiency Scores With Letter Grades. 101
　　　　Include Reperformances 102
　　　　Make the Gradebook an Active Part of Learning. 103
　　　　Ensure There Is Enough of the Right Evidence. 104
　　　　Assign Incompletes as Final Grades, if Needed. 104
　　　　Communicate Grades as Trends and Projections During Learning. 105
　　　　Assign Grades *After* Conversations With Students 106
　　　　Consider Homework as Evidence 106
　　　　Rethink the Format of Culminating Assessments 106
　　Conclusion. 107
　　Big-Impact Recommendations for Implementation 107

CHAPTER 10
Establish Dynamic Reporting Structures 109
　　Characteristics of a Dynamic Reporting Structure. 109
　　　　How Is the Student Growing? 112
　　　　How Is the Student Performing? 112
　　　　How Is the Student Behaving? 113

How Is the Student Preparing? 114
Conclusion. 117
Big-Impact Recommendations for Implementation 117
Homework Log *118*

Epilogue 119

A New Focus on the Student 119
Mission Statement Alignment 120
Curriculum Review 120
A New Look at Intervention 121
More Effective Collaboration Time 121
Conclusion. 121

References and Resources. 123

Index. 133

ABOUT THE AUTHORS

Anthony R. Reibel is director of assessment, research, and evaluation at Adlai E. Stevenson High School in Illinois. He administers assessments, manages student achievement data, and oversees instructional practice. Anthony began his professional career as a technology specialist and entrepreneur. After managing several businesses, he became a Spanish teacher at Stevenson. He has also served as a curricular team leader, core team leader, coach, and club sponsor.

In 2010, Anthony received recognition from the state of Illinois for Outstanding New Educator, and in 2011, the Illinois Computing Educators named him Technology Educator of the Year. He is a member of the Association for Supervision and Curriculum Development, Illinois Principals Association, Illinois Computing Educators, and American Council on the Teaching of Foreign Languages.

He earned a bachelor's degree in Spanish from Indiana University and master's degrees (one in curriculum and instruction and one in educational leadership) from Roosevelt University.

To learn more about Anthony's work, follow him @areibel on Twitter.

Matt Thede, MEd, is an assistant principal at Mount Vernon High School in Mount Vernon, Iowa. He is a former biology and Advanced Placement biology teacher at Prairie High School, in Cedar Rapids, Iowa, where he also led curricular improvements and professional development initiatives in the areas of standards-based grading, unit design, and instruction and assessment, and aligned those efforts with the district's progress as a professional learning community (PLC). After leaving professional baseball in 2003, Matt became an educator with a teaching background in science. His education experiences range from working in rural communities and school districts (Benton Community, Van Horne, Iowa) to urban and city districts (Prairie High School, Cedar Rapids, Iowa).

Matt has a strong belief in collaborating with and developing schools that desire to improve and respond to student needs, especially in the areas of grading, instruction, and assessment. He has also been a presenter at state standards-based conferences, speaking on the topics of evidence-based reporting and leading grading changes in secondary schools. He has a passion to help schools of any size and background implement lasting changes that positively impact student achievement with the resources they have.

Matt has consulted with several schools around the Midwest, taking his leadership and experiences from initiatives he's led and helping other schools do similar work. In addition, he was involved in working with gradebook developers to create a gradebook module that works for educators using standards-based practices.

Matt received a bachelor's degree in biology from Wartburg College, a master's degree in education from Graceland University, and a master's degree in educational leadership from Drake University.

To learn more about Matt's work, follow him @MattThede on Twitter.

To book Anthony R. Reibel or Matt Thede for professional development, contact pd@SolutionTree.com.

INTRODUCTION

A fundamental goal of education is to equip students with the self-regulatory capabilities that enable them to educate themselves.

—Albert Bandura

Matt Thede and a leadership team from Mount Vernon High School were about to enter Adlai E. Stevenson High School for the first time. Adlai E. Stevenson High School, or Stevenson as it's often referred to by those who know it, is in Lincolnshire, Illinois, a public high school with about four thousand students. It is a nationally recognized secondary high school and is informally known as the birthplace of Professional Learning Communities at Work® (PLCs at Work). To say Matt and his staff, small-town folk, felt a little overwhelmed and starstruck was an understatement.

There were several differences that Matt's team, as outsiders, noticed immediately. Stevenson is much larger than Mount Vernon. It averages close to one thousand students per graduating class, while Mount Vernon averages just around one hundred. Stevenson has more than three hundred staff members, while Mount Vernon has closer to thirty-five. Stevenson receives approximately two and one-half times more money per student than Mount Vernon gets from the state. These are just a few of the differences between the two schools that the team—we—were struck by.

We were met by Anthony Reibel, director of assessment, research, and evaluation at Stevenson, as he was going to be giving us our tour and walking us through some of the reforms Stevenson had been implementing. After the first part of the tour, we initially wondered if we would take anything away that would be relevant to the purpose of our trip. All the systems they had in place, along with the sheer number of people and resources present, made it initially feel like this was an apples and oranges comparison. Could a much smaller school with limited resources function at a level similar to Stevenson? Given the purpose of our trip was to explore PLC best practices and grading reform, we initially felt overwhelmed.

As we continued our visit, we started to realize the two schools had more things in common than what appeared at the onset. The size of Stevenson began to metaphorically shrink as we dug to the core of what we all believed was necessary for students to succeed. Stevenson was in the process of implementing sound instructional, assessment, and grading practices, and using PLCs as the framework by which to achieve that work. In addition, they had a solid student system to support all learners. Thoughts started crossing our minds about how we could take the supports and structures at Stevenson and apply them to Mount Vernon. We started down the path of imagining how we could adapt, assimilate, and arrange our resources to achieve similar reforms on our campus, only on a much smaller scale.

During this process, a simple truth emerged; Stevenson cemented its beliefs about teaching and learning, made them clear to all stakeholders, and built everything else around that foundation. The significant part is, core beliefs can be found in any school, of any size, in any district, including Mount Vernon. But in order to use core beliefs as a support system, it is necessary to articulate them, and to understand how they came about and what impact they have. Naturally, we started to think about our own core beliefs and how we could develop our systems to leverage those beliefs with the resources we had.

What started as a day to learn from Stevenson about PLCs quickly evolved into an examination of who we were as a high school and where we needed to go. And what started as a day with seemingly vast amounts of differences ended with recognition of common beliefs about teaching and learning that any school could take and apply to its context. It was the fact that many schools the size of Mount Vernon are looking for help with various parts of school reform and the assurance that schools of all sizes and shapes can implement common beliefs about teaching and learning that inspired us to write this book.

This book's purpose is to guide schools on how to make ten small-scale system changes that can have a significant impact on culture, learning, and relationships. These ten changes are rooted in core beliefs that value teaching as mentorship, the development of student self-efficacy and agency, and the importance of human connection. The ten changes require minimal resources to implement because they result from habits of mind and commitments.

About This Book

Although a school can read any chapter of this book and reform individual aspects of its campus, we placed the chapters in order for a reason, and we recommend walking through them one chapter at a time. This can help maximize implementation efforts; starting with and knowing the *why* drives purpose for such changes. There are ten changes that we have seen schools make, including our own, that have lead to positive, long-lasting change, each of which is covered in detail in a chapter of this book.

- **Chapter 1: Redefine student success**—In this chapter, we present the argument that schools should embrace efficacy as the universal definition of student success. Many schools continue to equate achievement with success. The higher a student's exam score or the more rigorous the course, the more educators and parents consider a student to be successful. However, the ability to sustain oneself in life pursuits and situations is far more predictive of a fulfilling and meaningful life (Bandura, 2012).

- **Chapter 2: Create student-centered mission statements**—Often, schools have mission statements focused on what they will do for the student, implicitly causing the student to rely on external support. In this chapter, you will learn that if schools have a student-centered, efficacious mission statement, they set themselves up for the right work, promoting self-reliance. Student-centered mission statements have an academic and social component to them, all the while promoting self-awareness and self-efficacy.

- **Chapter 3: Organize curriculum around skills, not content**—While standards are often established based on class content, we contend that curriculum should be organized around enduring, transferable skills. This chapter discusses the importance of centering curriculum around skills, allowing students to grow their self-efficacy as they transfer their learning from one class to another and into the world around them. Content is certainly valuable and needs to support students as they learn valuable, transferable, and enduring skills.

- **Chapter 4: Develop student-centered rubrics**—Today, most rubrics in education are used to communicate a grade or communicate a deficiency. This chapter offers strategies for developing student-centered rubrics that guide students toward the expected outcomes and, perhaps more important, allow students to see how well they are doing it. Student-centered rubrics are valuable resources and tools you can use to interact with students regarding their proficiency expectations.

- **Chapter 5: Use assessment as a process for learning**—This chapter explores assessment as part of instruction and contends they should occupy the same pedagogical space, being inseparable from one another. This allows assessments to be part of the process of learning, rather than a separate event in which to grade students. When teachers continually ask students to prove their knowledge throughout the learning process, they are more likely to develop self-sufficiency, learning how to validate and trust their thinking during a lesson.

- **Chapter 6: Implement a generative learning model of instruction**—We contend that teachers should use a generative model of learning and build on what students already know when designing an instructional model. This chapter explains how to build learning around mastery experiences that allow instruction, learning, assessment, and feedback to be interwoven and inseparable from one another. In this chapter, we model how a diamond lesson structure, or instructional diamond, can help implement a generative learning model of instruction.

- **Chapter 7: Provide critical, growth-based feedback**—It is no question that students gain great insight into their learning when teachers use prescriptive, growth-based feedback. In this chapter, we propose teachers should deliver feedback in a manner that describes a future course of action and invites students into the learning process and provides them with a foundation to grow their own learning toward the desired outcomes.

- **Chapter 8: Leverage reflection and reperformance**—In most classrooms, the need to cover a great deal of content within a limited time period can be a challenge. However, to make learning happen, it's important for teachers to make space for student reflection. In this chapter, we explore the idea of reflection and reperformance as essential elements of student learning and how teachers can find time in their busy day to offer these learning opportunities. When teachers provide space, it allows time for metacognition and self-deliberation to grow student thinking and learning.

- **Chapter 9: Use evidence-based grading practices**—In this chapter, we discuss how a student's total body of work (evidence from assessments collected over a grading period), along with consideration for growth throughout that particular learning cycle, should provide the evidence needed to determine accurate grading. When reported appropriately in the gradebook, these marks become an active part of the learning process and help propel students to grow and own it.

- **Chapter 10: Establish dynamic reporting structures**—The gradebook can play a crucial role in growing a student's learning if it clearly communicates the right information. This chapter describes how the gradebook can communicate stories of learning, inspire conversations, and promote self-evaluation. We recommend reporting (separately) how the student is growing, performing, behaving, and preparing. This gives all stakeholders clarity in seeing how the student is doing in each area and making appropriate actions to improve.

Each chapter ends with a section titled Big-Impact Recommendations for Implementation. Here, we offer possible next steps or reflection questions to help guide implementation as readers move forward with school reform. This provides guidance on how schools can get started with particular changes and reforms they are trying to make. Keep in mind, taking on one change at a time is a much more manageable approach than taking on multiple reforms all at the same time. This increases implementation fidelity and focus as you work toward a common goal.

A Final Thought

As educators implement any of these ten practices, students and teachers are more likely to feel a sense of community, engage in interpersonal connection, and develop a sense of personal agency.

Personal agency is often referred to as "the sources and levels of influence that mediate activity" (Smith, 2017, p. 67) and is fundamental to human behavior. Without agency, people may struggle to exercise influence over what they do. In other words, they might feel like they do not have the power to achieve goals, meet expectations, or produce positive outcomes (Bandura, 1997). Efficacy and agency are important for all people, but especially for students, and they are the foundational concepts of this book.

CHAPTER 1

Redefine Student Success

> *The bulk of U.S. education is a largely hollow process of temporarily retaining information required to get acceptable grades on tests.*
>
> —Tony Wagner and Ted Dintersmith

When educators ask us what their school can do to initiate lasting change, we typically respond by asking two questions, "Have you defined what success looks like for your students?" and "Do you have an accurate and calibrated perspective on what it means to learn?" In our experience, schools tend to overlook these questions as they focus their attention on daily practices. Although the analysis of classroom practices is essential, schools that explore these questions tend to have more success with school reform initiatives.

Before we explore these two questions more thoroughly, it is critically important to know the *why*, as it drives purpose for the content that follows. As we redefine student success, *self-efficacy* must be at the forefront of that definition, as it drives many of the small changes that have the potential for significant impact in your school. We encourage you to read the first two chapters as overarching educational philosophies to set the tone for the rest of the book. Redefining what student success looks like (chapter 1) and establishing a student-centered mission statement (chapter 2, page 15) are big-impact changes that will guide the rest of the changes throughout the book.

What Student Success Looks Like

Defining student success is a challenging task. Some educators may see achievement or the mastery of course material as a success for students, while others may consider success as the students' ability to learn despite hardships in their lives. Others may feel self-governance, self-regulation, and empathy are end goals of education, and for others still, success may mean something entirely different. Regardless of how we, as educators, determine student success, one common theme exists among many interpretations: self-efficacy.

Experts and researchers alike have been documenting the connection between self-efficacy and personal well-being for decades. We can generally think of *personal efficacy* as self-reliance (Bandura, 1997). Many experts consider the development of personal efficacy as paramount to one being able to function as a responsible adult citizen, as it correlates to many health and wellness benefits such as right actions and choices, increased effort, perseverance, ability to handle adversity, healthy thought patterns, lower stress and depression, and increased level of realized accomplishments (Bandura, 1997; Johnson, Johnson-Pynn, Drescher, Sackey, & Assenga, 2019; Maddux & Kleiman, 2016). In one study, Albert Bandura and Robert Wood (1989) demonstrate that efficacy is a more significant contributor to life satisfaction and realized achievement than IQ, race, and socioeconomic status. To this end, we suggest that any school looking to make any kind of reform start by defining success for students as efficacy development.

Guidelines for Redefining Success

Education is the perfect opportunity for a student to begin to develop his or her efficacy and self-reliance. Much of the research supports the notion that the higher one's efficacy, the stronger the motivation, confidence, and drive to learn (Artino, 2012; Maddux & Stanley, 1986). The lower one's efficacy, the more apathy and indifference toward learning (Bandura, 1986). To help ensure that your definition of student success is aligned with efficacy development, consider the following five criteria when creating your definition of student success.

1. Positive self-concept
2. Self-sustenance
3. Accurate perception of abilities
4. Social connection and emotional awareness
5. Articulation and communication

Positive Self-Concept

Connecting learning with student identity is essential to their success. Education expert Jere Brophy (2008) asserts that research as far back as the early twentieth century finds that when students show a genuine interest in learning, it is due to an identification of the self with a concept. In other words, students who can view course content in the context of who they are and what they care about have more intrinsic motivation and more eagerness to learn (Flum & Kaplan, 2012).

Brophy (2008) also states that the classroom curriculum must come into alignment with students' internal interests and values for real engagement in classroom learning to occur. In other words, the classroom curriculum must provide some form of relevance to students' lives.

Schools should help students pay attention not only to the classroom environment but to their perceptions of themselves in it (Ketelsen, 2017). You can help students discover who they are by encouraging them to feel personally connected to what they do in school (Faircloth, 2012). If you allow students to access their non-school identities during learning (such as identities with origins in family, culture, and community), you may see higher student achievement as well as increased engagement.

Self-Sustenance

When students are more accurately aware of the nature of their abilities, they are more likely to be accepting of who they are (Bandura, 2018). With this acceptance, they can better self-sustain through challenges, self-direct toward goals, and remediate difficulties. Insight into who they are enables students to participate in the classroom more effectively because they tend to be more accepting of themselves and can better examine and develop their strengths. Ultimately, it is through an education that students begin to develop this trust of what works in their learning along with a trust in themselves to grow in what doesn't work. This doesn't just apply to education, but life as well. In other words, if I "know myself," I can "grow myself."

When you give students the proper feedback and permission to learn (without fear of a grade in the gradebook), they can build intellectual and emotional resiliency that will help them in school and life situations.

You should aim to create environments that embrace failure without the consequence of punishment. Consequence-free exploration and productive failure can help students avoid *failure deprivation* (Hibbs & Rostain, 2019). Students who have been deprived of failure by their teachers or parents may create a false sense of mastery that, if exposed, leads to adverse emotional reactions, such as anxiety, anger, and depression, among others (Bandura, 2018).

Accurate Perception of Abilities

Education can be a safe place for a student to realize his or her actual abilities in the context of the larger world. When students experience failure, they are more likely to gain an accurate perception of who they are and who they could be (Zimmerman, Bandura, & Martinez-Pons, 2011). Students who explore the thresholds of their abilities honestly and accurately begin to develop better self-regulatory skills (Schwarzer, 2015).

To help students gain more insight into their abilities, it is essential to create intentional pauses in your lessons to allow for student self-deliberation and reflection (see chapter 8, page 89, for more information). One way you can create these *pauses* is by stopping a lesson and having students answer a few reflective questions, such as, "Are you where you are supposed to be in the learning? How do you know?" or "If I (the teacher) were to look at your work thus far, what do you think I would say about it?" These questions are just a few examples that can help make the student look inward.

Looking inward consists of important self-regulatory capabilities—self-deliberation and self-appraisal. Bandura (1997) finds that specific breaks for introspection during the learning process can help students become acutely aware of their strengths and weaknesses. In addition, Anne Graham and Robyn Fitzgerald (2010) find that students are less likely to develop despondency if they confront the realities of their performances though moments of self-appraisal. For example, consider the three students in figure 1.1.

	Student A	**Student B**	**Student C**
Standard X	3	4	1
Standard Y	1	1	1
Standard Z	3	3	1
	Student A scored himself inaccurately in standard Y.	Student B scored herself inaccurately in each standard.	Student C scored himself accurately in each standard.

Figure 1.1: Student self-appraisal of standards.

Now, consider this question, Which student is the most important for you to speak to first? Student C, who has major deficits in all standards? Student A, who scored himself inaccurately in standard Y? Or student B, who scored herself inaccurately in all standards?

We contend that student B is the most urgent to speak with, as she has an inaccurate appraisal of her abilities. If student B was left to perform tasks with an inaccurate perception of her abilities, it could prove cognitively and emotionally problematic when these tasks call for abilities that she thought she had but in reality did not. This realization could manifest itself in maladaptive reactions, such as acting out, engaging defense mechanisms, disregarding feedback, or displaying avoidance behaviors (Hibbs & Rostain, 2019).

Social Connection and Emotional Awareness

A better sense of who they are can help students gain the ability to connect socially as well as develop better awareness of their emotions (emotional acuity), which are traits students need as they develop into mature and independent adults (Zimmerman et al., 2011).

Christopher Emdin (2016), author of *For White Folks Who Teach in the Hood . . . and the Rest of Y'all Too*, states that a student's "relationship to emotional space is a constitutive part of their existence" (p. 26). Emdin (2016) goes on to say that until teachers respect the emotions of their students and see them as valuable to the learning process, students may remain invisible to teachers. In other words, if a student is producing successful academic results, the teacher may still make assumptions about a student's learning and potentially miss opportunities to help him or her. This same literature suggests that when intervention and student support programs help students to better access their non-school identities—identities that contain many of their emotional realities, such as family, culture, and community—their achievement and engagement increase (Ketelsen, 2017).

Articulation and Communication

Work hard to gather first-person accounts from students about their learning. Unless students are able to clearly articulate their learning needs, you will be more likely to make assumptions about students' learning profiles. For example, don't say, "You got these three questions wrong; you need to work on (content or skill)." Instead, give the student the opportunity to articulate any context about the situation, either through writing or speaking. For example, you might say, "I noticed that you got these three questions wrong. What might have happened?" or "What were you feeling and thinking here? Were you feeling confident, confused, unsure, or something else?"

This approach not only provides the space for students to communicate their learning but also shows that you value their inner world. When you show students that you truly want to hear what they think and feel, a more trusting learning relationship develops between teacher and student.

What Student Learning Looks Like

Some educators tend to view learning as transactional. Transactional learning goes something like this: the teacher teaches content and skills, while the students demonstrate retention of content and skills, and the teacher awards points for accuracy. But perhaps there is another way to view learning. We have seen schools have more success when they consider learning not as a transactional process but as a generative process (Brown, Roediger, & McDaniel, 2014). Researchers Hanoch Flum and Avi Kaplan (2012) say teachers can better support learners by examining their perspectives on what it means to learn. Figure 1.2 shows a visual representation of generative learning.

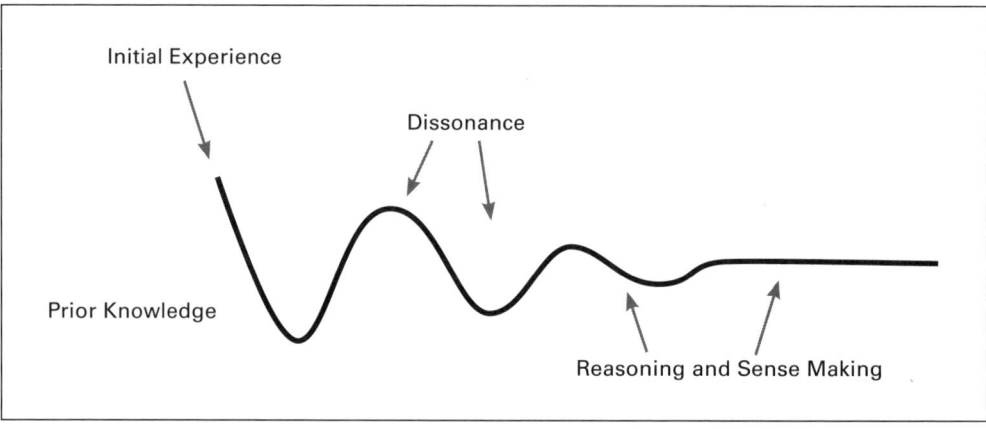

Figure 1.2: Visual representation of generative learning.

Having a generative perspective of learning engages students in performance first; then teachers react to their performance by providing guidance, feedback, and evaluation.

Guidelines for Defining Learning

When teachers espouse the perspective of learning reflected in figure 1.2, instruction and assessment tend to focus on the following qualities of lifelong learning.

- Personal agency
- Generative learning
- Rooted competence
- Constructive failure

Personal Agency

Too often, students are not able to self-direct due to the constrictive structure of traditional schooling. They attend schools that reward compliance and may struggle with creating and thinking for themselves. When students self-navigate, they begin to feel more in control of their learning and to use this feeling of personal agency to make new connections and insights. The more power students feel over their social and academic competencies, the more confident they become in their ability to achieve goals. They are also more likely to participate more confidently in social settings and can develop more personally rewarding relationships (Zimmerman et al., 2011).

To help students develop personal agency, you can develop experiences and assessments that require self-reliance. When school leaders ask teachers to add components of self-navigation to their pedagogy, it can provide an opportunity for students to improve personal agency.

Generative Learning

When teachers help students become active agents of their learning, this leads to more competent material application and lasting proficiency (Bandura, 2012). If we plan lessons aligned with the true nature of learning, we see lessons *generate* rather than *deliver* learning. These lessons would see the teacher *reacting* to student evidence and using student thinking as lesson material. These lesson designs would include individual reflection, consensus, sense making, perspective creation, and proficiency development. When you approach lesson design with generative learning in mind, you can create lessons that are more dynamic, malleable, and reactive to students' learning needs.

Rooted Competence

We want students to attain *enduring* learning, skills, and knowledge that is rooted in long-term memory. According to Bandura (1997), "Most competencies must be developed over a long period. For complex ones, different subskills must be acquired, integrated, and hierarchically organized under continually changing conditions that can enhance or mar particular performances" (p. 86). No teacher knows how long it takes a student to learn a concept or skill. To this end, lessons are more effective if they allow for real-time reactions and adjustments to student learning instead of cycling through preplanned activities (Brown et al., 2014).

Constructive Failure

Educators need to design instruction that supports and sometimes even invites failure. In their book *Developing Assessment-Capable Visible Learners, Grades K–12: Maximizing Skill, Will, and Thrill*, Nancy Frey, John Hattie, and Douglas

Fisher (2018) discuss the difference between unproductive and productive failure. Unproductive failure is when someone shows the inability to learn or grow from their errors, while productive failure is learning from errors and persisting in generating and exploring one's learning (Frey et al., 2018). Many researchers (Brown et al., 2014; Carey, 2014) now articulate that learning is more a process of development, failure, and refinement. Because initial learning is unsteady and fluctuating (Jain & Reibel, 2018), students need to learn that failure is a valuable part of learning.

Conclusion

Our hope in this chapter was to help you look at your current definition of student success and ensure that self-efficacy is a part of that definition. For example, Mount Vernon redefined student success by looking at students' exit outcomes. It asked the valuable question, "What do we want students to look like when they leave Mount Vernon?" They wanted students to have high self-efficacy; learn valuable, transferable skills; and be great communicators. This redefined what student success looked like for them and would serve as the foundation by which all other pedagogical work would take place.

Big-Impact Recommendations for Implementation

Perhaps one of the best ways to redefine student success is to gather stakeholders and leaders in your school and community in a roundtable setting and ask the following questions: "What do we want our students to look like as they leave our school? What characteristics do we want them to possess?" Refer to the following guiding points and questions as you reflect on the information in this chapter.

1. Be sure that pedagogical practices match the true nature of learning.
   Key question—Do our instruction and assessment practices align with the image of learning in figure 1.2 (page 12)? Do we understand that failure isn't always represented with a letter grade of F, but is a valuable part of learning?

2. Create opportunities to learn from failure.
   Key question—Do our instructional activities and assessments promote productive student actions and responses?

3. Do not define student success as *achievement only*.
   Key question—Does our definition of student success include self-reliance, commitment to community, and a respect for learning?

CHAPTER 2

Create Student-Centered Mission Statements

A mission statement should act as the figurehead of the school. It should be a call to action, describing the purpose of why the school exists, what its goals are, and what its potential contributions to the community may be.

—Richard DuFour

It is common knowledge that a mission statement states a school's primary purpose as the preparation of students to be functioning citizens and well-rounded human beings. Perhaps Tony Wagner and Ted Dintersmith (2015) say it best:

> We believe that the start point for taking on the fundamental question of 'What is the purpose of education?' is that education needs to help youth discover their passions and purpose in life, develop the critical skills necessary to be successful in pursuing their goals, be inspired on a daily basis to do their very best, and be active and informed citizens. Without this foundation, schools will continue to fall short. (p. 44)

The problem we see with many mission statements is that they imply that students should rely on the school to make them lifelong learners instead of themselves. A mission statement can sound something like, "We will foster lifelong learners . . . " or "We will prepare our students for the next phase of their lives . . . " When schools explicitly, or implicitly, communicate that they are primarily responsible for students' learning and growth, students might become overly reliant on external support and reinforcement for their success. To help keep students from interpreting mission statements in this way, schools should ensure that their mission statements *focus on the student.*

Characteristics of a Student-Centered Mission Statement

A student-centered mission statement focuses on the student's growth, self-reliant habits and behaviors, and a goal of self-reliance. For example, Mount Vernon uses the following student-centered mission statement: *Fostering growth and confidence as learners and people in society.* Not only does it have an academic and social component, but it also promotes student self-awareness (growth) and self-efficacy (confidence).

Student-centered mission statements might include the following themes:

- Academic acuity and interest
- Social connection
- Emotional awareness and self-concept
- Self-efficacy

Academic Acuity and Interest

Academic acuity and interest go hand in hand. In their 2011 study, researchers Jason W. Osborne and Brett D. Jones found that when students struggle academically, it may be due to a lack of perceived value in the subject rather than a lack of ability. In their study, they found that to the extent to which a student values the subject correlates to the extent to which he or she is motivated to learn (Osborne & Jones, 2011). Students who realize consistent early successes are more likely to maintain interest in the course material.

When you seek to understand the level to which your students identify with the course material and classroom environment, it provides you with insights into students' performance. When you understand how much students value the course material, it can increase the likelihood that students achieve initial success in these courses and an increasing interest in the content.

Social Connection

Another theme that should be present in a student-centered mission statement is a student's sense of belonging. Many experts find that there is a positive association between a sense of belonging in the classroom and the quality of a student's learning experience (Faircloth, 2012; St.-Amand, Girard, & Smith, 2017).

Researchers Lisa Fast and colleagues (2010) find that students who have the perception that their teacher cares about them tend to perform better on standardized exams. A student's sense of belonging can also determine whether students stay in school or drop out (Adams-Byers, Whitsell, & Moon, 2004).

However, there is research that finds disconcerting evidence regarding academic challenge and belonging (Adams-Byers et al., 2004). This research suggests that students may encounter negative stereotypes. Common stereotypes include African American students not being as intelligent as white students (Gates & Steele, 2009), or males being better at science than females (McGuire et al., 2020). Some studies even indicate that when students use stereotypes involving gender and academic abilities, such as *boys are smarter than girls*, it can negatively impact girls' test scores in all areas, but more often in mathematics and engineering (McGuire et al., 2020).

To this end, schools should be very careful and specific when creating mission statements. To be truly student-centered, a mission statement should exclude no one and communicate that relationships of any kind are valued.

Emotional Awareness and Self-Concept

Connecting learning with student identity is essential to success, and mission statements are one of the ways to help students understand this point. Researcher Beverly Faircloth (2012) finds that this type of connection is critical to positive learning. She studied a diverse group of ninth-grade students who were struggling in their English classes. She found that a student's identity is negotiated during learning. In other words, *learning and identity formation* are reciprocal tasks for students.

To this end, students who examine the relevance of course content that connects to them in some way are more likely to develop intrinsic motivation and show an increase in eagerness to learn (Flum & Kaplan, 2012).

Student-centered mission statements should help students learn to pay attention not only to the classroom environment but also to how they perceive themselves in it (Ketelsen, 2017). A student with more emotional awareness may be more apt to say, "I know I can't do algebra right now, but I understand if I take certain steps, I can learn it."

Self-Efficacy

Zimmerman et al. (2011) define *self-efficacy* as one's belief in his or her ability to succeed in specific situations or accomplish a task. In their research, they found causal links between self-efficacy and learning, such as increased feedback acceptance, more meaningful self-reflection, and more accurate self-assessment, to name a few.

John Hattie (2012), laureate professor at the University of Melbourne, Australia, has been able to highlight the impact of efficacious learning traits. Through his in-depth meta-analysis, he finds that a student's efficacy has an effect size of 0.92 on his or her learning. Keep in mind that Hattie (2012) claims anything above 0.40 has an impact on student learning, so a 0.92 appears to be significant.

The higher the efficacy, the stronger the motivation, confidence, and drive to learn (Maddux, 1995). The connection between well-being and realized achievement and efficacy was theorized by many, including Roger D. Goddard, Wayne K. Hoy, and Anita Woolfolk Hoy (2000) and Bandura (2012). Zimmerman et al. (2011) show the correlation between efficacy, achievement, and social-emotional development. The lower the efficacy, the more apathy and indifference students have toward learning (Zimmerman et al., 2011).

In some studies, efficacy has been shown to be more important in explaining life satisfaction and realized achievement than intelligence, race, and socioeconomic status (Bandura, 1997). With all of this said, and because of its connection to well-being in adulthood, themes of efficacy should be included in mission statements.

How to Develop Student-Centered Mission Statements

When teachers plan lessons, they start with the end in mind (Wiggins & McTighe, 2011). In other words, what should students know and be able to do? When it comes to mission statements, school leaders should do the same. Student-centered, efficacy-focused mission statements should describe graduates who possess personal agency, self-reliance, and social-emotional competence. Schools can develop mission statements with a more specific student focus by making sure they embrace the following five characteristics.

1. Values self-reliant learning
2. Guards against transient learning
3. Doesn't make assumptions about student learning
4. Avoids common misperceptions about student learning
5. Uses student-produced evidence to make decisions

The following example mission statement is adapted from Stevenson's portrait of a graduate. As you read the the sections that follow, see if this mission statement holds up to the five previously listed characteristics.

Mission statement: Developing self-sufficient learners who have respect for self, respect for community, and respect for learning.

Values Self-Reliant Learning

When schools include a message of self-reliance in their mission statements, they remind everyone that the school values independent student learning. They communicate that they aim to produce learners who take personal ownership over their learning, possess a shared responsibility for their decisions, and emanate hope. Walking the halls of these schools, one may hear students discussing problems in mathematics class, supporting friends, or debating the next steps in their school career. In these schools, students don't spend time in the hall avoiding classes, scribbling homework to get it done, or sitting alone in the lunchroom.

Guards Against Transient Learning

Mission statements should communicate that the school values a genuine demonstration of skills and knowledge. Schools with these mission statements strive to foster student learning that is fully mature and rooted. Mission statements that promote self-efficacy and guard against transient learning invite teachers to take a mentoring role in the learning process. In mentoring roles, teachers can better transfer their efficacious traits to students (Bandura, 1997), for example, analytical thinking, logical problem solving, and self-regulation.

In our sample mission statement, we find the words *respect for learning*. This phrase asks teachers to create learning environments where students have adequate time and multiple opportunities to build fully developed competence in all course skills and standards. When students truly have the skills to learn, they feel more confident and in control of their lives (Bandura, 1997).

Doesn't Make Assumptions About Student Learning

When using forced-choice assessments, teacher-centered instruction, or impersonal grading practices, one may make assumptions about student learning. For example, if a student includes all criteria from the rubric, how do you know his or her performance isn't just mimicry? If you are too heavily involved in a lesson, how can you know for sure that a student can independently apply the knowledge? Or if a student gets a question correct, how do you know he or she didn't guess? These are critical questions that school leaders can address with a student-centered, efficacy-based mission statement.

In our sample mission statement, we find that the terms *self-sufficient* and *respect for learning* call on teachers to make student thinking a norm in their classrooms. When students see their thought processes as reliable, they are more likely to develop a more accurate perception of their abilities. This accurate perception is paramount to self-sufficiency.

Avoids Common Misperceptions About Student Learning

When schools create mission statements that commit stakeholders to developing the students' self-appraisal abilities, they can better promote pedagogy that encourages student empowerment. When students are empowered, they are more likely to be in tune with their learning thresholds, their limitations, or their emotional responses to performances and feedback.

Our sample mission statement contains the phrase *respect for community* and captures what we have just described. Researchers continue to find that the more accurate the perception of self that people have, the more in control they feel of their lives. The more personal control one feels, the more likely he or she is to actively participate in society (Schwarzer, 2015).

Uses Student-Produced Evidence to Make Decisions

Any mentor knows that to assess a mentee, he or she needs sufficient evidence. Take baseball, for example. A coach would be shortsighted to judge a hitter's ability based on one at bat. The better practice would be for a coach to use the total of many at bats to help the batter make proper adjustments and validate his or her mechanics.

In the same way, student-centered mission statements call on schools to use only relevant and reliable evidence of learning. These schools have classrooms in which students engage in mastery experiences that produce undeniable evidence from which all stakeholders can make decisions and policy. Although student-produced evidence may not be as tidy as points, averages, or percentages, it provides information that underscores objective feedback, meaningful communication, and final grades.

To review, let's analyze several mission statements using the five characteristics previously described to see if they are student-centered. Figure 2.1 shows several sample mission statements. Review each statement, determine whether it is student-centered, and list your reasons why or why not.

Mission Statement	Student-Centered?	Reasons
Success for Every Student	Yes Sort of No	
We strive to create a safe and inspiring school experience where students become thoughtful learners, active citizens, and confident leaders through quality educational experiences that promote critical thinking, civic responsibility, and personal development.	Yes Sort of No	
Preparing every student for success in post-secondary academics, career, and life.	Yes Sort of No	
We ensure every student reaches his or her full potential.	Yes Sort of No	

Figure 2.1: Sample mission statements.

Conclusion

Student-based mission statements represent authentic and compassionate cultures in our schools. The message of a mission statement should be alive in the voices and actions of every participant in the school community. Mission statements should be a reminder to all that the purpose of school is to prepare the next generation of humans to have high self-efficacy and be self-sufficient and compassionate citizens of the world. To make this happen, stakeholders should continually reflect on its message and ensure it doesn't become *just* a banner on the wall.

Big-Impact Recommendations for Implementation

When creating student-centered mission statements, we recommend working with a student improvement advisory committee of invested stakeholders, such as administrators, teachers, parents, community members, and students. As you work through what it means to have a student-centered mission statement, remember it should value self-reliant learning, guard against transient learning, not make assumptions about student learning, avoid common misperceptions about student learning, and use student-produced evidence to make decisions.

Refer to the following guiding points and questions as you reflect on the information in this chapter.

1. Mission statements should focus more on students than on teacher practices.
   Key question—Does your mission statement contain student-centered themes and language?

2. Mission statements should focus on themes of self-reliance and empowerment.
   Key question—Does your mission statement contain themes of personal efficacy and personal agency?

3. Mission statements should guide a school's culture and pedagogy.
   Key question—Is your mission statement a living document used throughout the year by all stakeholders?

CHAPTER 3

Organize Curriculum Around Skills, Not Content

Academic skills—such as mastery of reading, math, and science—are crucial but not sufficient. Young people increasingly need to be able to do such things as develop ideas, empathize with others, and collaboratively problem-solve; they also need to have the resilience and adaptability to continue to learn and master new things.

—Rebecca Winthrop and Eileen McGivney

More often than not, educators use the definition of *standard* in the fixed, limited sense of what the student must know and be able to do. However, another definition of *standard* evokes a focus on the iterative changes that are part of learning. A standard can also refer to a tool for measuring quality. This emphasis on quality focuses on the learning process rather than just on results.

If we consider these two definitions as valuable, we must focus on results *and* process and quality. Consider a phrase like *I can write, solve, and analyze linear equations in one variable.* In a limited sense of the word, this is a *standard*, but it does not address quality and the process of learning. Now consider the statement *I can effectively write, solve, and analyze equations in any mathematical context.* This is standard in the true sense of the word because it speaks to the level, or quality, of attainment. The terms *linear* and *one variable* from the first example should serve as *criteria* for meeting the standard, not the standard itself. And in the second example, the words *effectively* and *any mathematical context* act as the outline of how well the action is to be done.

We suggest using this information when you are developing curriculum. There are three ways you can do this.

1. Create a skills-based curricular structure.
2. Know the difference between proficiency gradations and learning progressions. Use the former for evaluation and the latter for instruction.
3. Differentiate between recursive and nonrecursive criteria.

Create a Skills-Based Curricular Structure

No matter if from the national, state, or district level, all curricula have a similar structure. This structure is commonly organized into content, topics, concepts, and skills, in no particular order (Gobble, Onuscheck, Reibel, & Twadell, 2016). For example, the Next Generation Science Standards include science practices and cross-cutting concepts, while the Common Core State Standards for Mathematics include a section that describes the essential mathematical practices. We support these inclusions; however, they are usually side notes or footnotes. Instead, these skills should be the focal point of curriculum development. To do this, we suggest that you keep the following four priority focuses in mind.

1. Start with enduring, transferable skills.
2. Create a standard or standards for each skill.
3. Develop proficiency gradations for each standard.
4. Set criteria for each proficiency gradation.

Start With Enduring, Transferable Skills

Typically, three to seven skills per course (for example, in English language arts, reading, writing, speaking, and listening) are enduring, transferable skills that students should develop by the end of a course (Guskey, 2013). Three to seven skills is an appropriate number, as it makes for the right range for effective communication; too many skills become overwhelming, and too few don't communicate enough information.

In order to leverage vertically aligned teams and ensure students reach necessary proficiencies by the conclusion of their secondary education, we emphasize that schools teach skills in the same skill areas in middle school as they do in high school. For example, in high school English, we use reading, writing, and speaking and listening as our three skill categories across grades 9–12. These should also be the skill areas taught across grades 5–8 so that skill acquisition happens on a continuum. Figure 3.1 shows what teachers might use in a mathematics course.

| 1. Create Mathematical Representations (Problem Solving) | 2. Simplify, Solve, and Evaluate (Computing) | 3. Analyze and Interpret (Justifying) |

Figure 3.1: Example of enduring, transferable mathematics skills.

Once you have defined the enduring skills of your course, it is time to set the level of quality expected for each skill.

Create a Standard or Standards for Each Skill

At stated earlier, a standard is typically a statement of how well a student should perform the skill to be considered competent. Figure 3.2 is an example of how standards align with the skills.

1. Create Mathematical Representations (Problem Solving)	2. Simplify, Solve, and Evaluate (Computing)	3. Analyze and Interpret (Justifying)
I can effectively create visual and symbolic representations.	I can correctly simplify, solve, and evaluate expressions, equations, or inequalities.	I can make viable arguments and decisions.

Figure 3.2: Example of standards for mathematics skills.

Figure 3.3 (page 26) shows another example of skill and standard alignment for English language arts. Notice there are *what* and *how well* components for each standard in alignment with the skill.

1. Writing (Skill)	2. Language (Skill)
A. Writing (standard) I can produce clear and coherent writing in which the development and organization are appropriate to task, purpose, and audience. **B. Narrative Writing (standard)** I can write narratives about real or imagined events using sensory details and event sequences (transitions), along with introductions and conclusions. **C. Opinion Writing (standard)** I can write a personal opinion paragraph about a given or chosen topic or text with a clear opinion supported by reasons.	**A. Grammar and Convention Usage (standard)** I can write a paragraph using grade-appropriate grammar rules and writing conventions effectively and accurately.

Source: ©2019 by Cathy Steines. Used with permission.

Figure 3.3: Example of skill and standard alignment for English language arts.

As you can see from these examples, when written correctly, standards help students gain a clearer picture of what is expected of them.

Develop Proficiency Gradations for Each Standard

Standard proficiency gradations inherently focus on the question, How well is a student expected to demonstrate his or her new learning? (Sandrock, 2011). Proficiency gradations communicate high expectations for students, let teachers use meaningful and specific feedback, and, most important, outline a road map for student learning.

These gradations outline the levels of competence relative to the standard; sometimes these are referred to as *proficiency scales*. We suggest a four-level gradation, although we acknowledge that the use of other gradations is plausible. The four levels we recommend are: (4) exceeds grade-level standard, (3) meets standard, (2) approaching standard, and (1) still developing foundational skills. Figure 3.4 shows examples of proficiency gradations across content areas.

Mathematics Skill: Mathematical Representations

Exceeds Grade-Level Standard (4)	Meets Standard (3)	Approaching Standard (2)	Still Developing Foundational Skills (1)
I can create an accurate visual or symbolic representation in any given context in unfamiliar situations.	I can create an accurate visual or symbolic representation in any given context.	I can create an appropriate visual or symbolic representation.	I can attempt to create a visual or symbolic representation.

Source: ©2016 Adlai E. Stevenson High School Mathematics Department. Used with permission.

English Language Arts Skill: Argumentation

Exceeds Grade-Level Standard (4)	Meets Standard (3)	Approaching Standard (2)	Still Developing Foundational Skills (1)
I can create an effective and original argument communicated in written form, acknowledging diverse perspectives, to support a claim and counterclaim, with reasons and the use of complex evidence.	I can create an effective and original argument communicated in written form to support a claim and address a counterclaim, with reasons and credible evidence from multiple perspectives.	I can create an original argument communicated in written form to support a claim, with basic reasons and the use of credible evidence.	I can attempt to create an argument communicated in written form to support a claim, using credible or non-credible reasons and evidence.

Science Skill: Data Interpretation and Analysis

Exceeds Grade-Level Standard (4)	Meets Standard (3)	Approaching Standard (2)	Still Developing Foundational Skills (1)
I can accurately interpret and analyze data and/or text in unfamiliar contexts.	I can accurately interpret and analyze data and/or text in different contexts.	I can interpret and analyze data and/or text in different contexts with some success.	I can interpret parts of data and/or text in different contexts with support.

Source: ©2018 by Mount Vernon High School Science Team. Used with permission.

Figure 3.4: Proficiency gradations across content areas.   *continued →*

Social Studies Skill: Source Evaluation

Exceeds Grade-Level Standard (4)	Meets Standard (3)	Approaching Standard (2)	Still Developing Foundational Skills (1)
I can accurately critique the credibility of multiple types of sources by corroborating, noting evidentiary limitations, and determining their relevance and intended use.	I can accurately critique the credibility of a source by corroborating, noting evidentiary limitations, and determining its relevance and intended use.	I can critique the credibility of a source by corroborating and determining its relevance or intended use.	I can attempt to critique the credibility of a source.

Source: ©2019 by Mount Vernon High School Social Studies Team. Used with permission.

Thomas R. Guskey (2013) contends that as more levels of gradation are added, the more likely students are to be misclassified in terms of their performance. As the number of gradations increase, there is less chance teachers would be able to rank a student similarly. We maintain that a four-point gradation promotes more powerful feedback. Some teachers are tempted to let the scale itself offer the feedback by adding in more and more gradations to give what they feel is a more precise marker of a student's proficiency level. However, by letting more levels of gradations speak *for* them, teachers offer feedback that is of lower quality and less personal.

As we will go on to explain throughout this book, proficiency gradations are an essential part of assessment, instruction, feedback, and grading.

Set Criteria for Each Proficiency Gradation

All standards have criteria that outline the necessary components a student needs to use to demonstrate competence. Content and prerequisite skills typically reside here. These criteria can be recursive (consistent all semester) or nonrecursive (different unit by unit). Figures 3.5, 3.6, and 3.7 (pages 29–30) show examples of success criteria you can use to help students see where they are at on the scale (gradation of learning).

Organize Curriculum Around Skills, Not Content

Career and Technical Education (CTE)

Skill: Automotive Technology—Tools and Equipment Mechanics			
Exceeds Grade-Level Standard (4)	**Meets Standard (3)**	**Approaching Standard (2)**	**Still Developing Foundational Skills (1)**
I always select and use the correct basic hand tools and equipment for vehicle repairs.	I correctly select and use basic hand tools and shop equipment for vehicle repairs.	I select and use basic hand tools and equipment for vehicle repairs.	I attempt to select and use basic hand tools and equipment for vehicle repairs.
Success Criteria: • Identify and measure metric and standard fasteners. • Correctly identify and use basic hand tools. • Identify and demonstrate the use of basic measuring tools. • Use reference manuals or information systems to find service procedures and specifications. • Properly raise and support vehicles using jack stands and a frame contact hoist.			

Source: ©2018 by Ben Kuker. Used with permission.

Figure 3.5: Automotive technology skill with supporting success criteria.

Science: Chemistry

Skill: Modeling			
Exceeds Grade-Level Standard (4)	**Meets Standard (3)**	**Approaching Standard (2)**	**Still Developing Foundational Skills (1)**
I can interpret or construct an effective model in an unfamiliar context using all relevant key features.	I can interpret or construct an effective model in a familiar context using all relevant key features.	I can interpret or construct a model in a familiar context with some key features.	I can interpret or construct a model in a familiar context with support.

Figure 3.6: Science skill with supporting success criteria.

continued →

> **Success Criteria:**
> - Use multiple types of models to support scientific explanations.
> - Create, revise, and use models to support scientific explanations.
> - Use models to predict, analyze, and solve problems.
> - Develop models that test a proposed problem.
> - Create models that include appropriate terms and are scientifically accurate.

Source: ©2018 by Mount Vernon High School Science Team. Adapted with permission.

Social Studies

Skill: Pattern Recognition			
Exceeds Grade-Level Standard (4)	**Meets Standard (3)**	**Approaching Standard (2)**	**Still Developing Foundational Skills (1)**
I can evaluate patterns of continuity and change over time within and across cultures, as well as distinguish causation, using relevant evidence.	I can evaluate patterns of continuity and change over time within and across cultures using relevant evidence.	I can evaluate patterns of continuity and change over time within and across cultures using relevant and non-relevant evidence.	I can attempt to evaluate patterns of continuity and change over time within and across cultures using a prompt.

> **Success Criteria:**
> - I can address multiple causes of the event.
> - I can address impacts (long term and immediate) of the event.
> - I can compare and contrast similar events in history.
> - I can identify and use key concepts that go with the time period.
> - I can determine the causes and effects of historical and contemporary events.
> - I can gather and use relevant evidence.
> - I can understand and include context.

Source: ©2019 by Brian Nichols and Brett Moorman. Adapted with permission.

Figure 3.7: Social studies skill with supporting success criteria.

Organize Curriculum Around Skills, Not Content

Success criteria play a crucial role in allowing students to see what they need to learn and apply to achieve proficiency on a particular skill. Without these criteria, students will have a hard time contextualizing the language in the proficiency gradation. We find that students who receive both the proficiency gradations and the associated success criteria from their teachers have an easier time understanding what is expected of them.

Know the Difference Between Proficiency Gradations and Learning Progressions

In the previous examples, you might have noticed the verbs in the proficiency scales were the same from one level to the next; this is called a proficiency (or learning) gradation. Proficiency gradations maintain the same verb in each level, but the modifying language is changed to communicate the level of mastery expected. For example, in figure 3.7, each proficiency gradation begins with *I can evaluate*. In contrast, learning progressions use a different verb with each level, ranging from simple application or depth of knowledge to more complex application or depth of knowledge. In figure 3.7, it would become a learning progression if we change the verb in each level, something like: *I can explain, I can evaluate, I can define*, or *I can list*.

The issue we see is that some teachers attempt to implement a skills-based curriculum with learning progressions instead of proficiency gradations. While learning progressions are effective for instructional purposes, a skills-based curriculum is more effective when it is based on proficiency gradations.

Figure 3.8 shows an example of a proficiency gradation compared with a learning progression.

Learning Progression
4—*Analyze* familiar and structured situations using appropriate vocabulary, context, and details.
3—*Explain* the relevant details in familiar and structured situations.
2—*Define* the appropriate vocabulary, details, and context in familiar and structured situations.
1—*Identify* the appropriate vocabulary, details, and context in familiar and structured situations.

Figure 3.8: Proficiency gradation compared with a learning progression.   *continued →*

Proficiency Gradation
4 — *Independently create* an appropriate spoken message in unfamiliar and unstructured situations.
3 — *Independently create* an appropriate spoken message in familiar and unstructured situations.
2 — *Independently create* an appropriate spoken message in familiar and structured situations.
1 — *Independently attempt to create* an appropriate spoken message in familiar and structured situations.

To highlight the point further, let's explore the concept of shadows. When people think about shadows, they usually think about what is known as *cast shadows*, which are the shadows directly behind the object (see figure 3.9).

Figure 3.9: Light reflecting off a ball.

There is a gradation of dark black to light black to dark grey to light grey. Now, let's apply this same concept to understanding the difference between proficiency gradations and learning progressions. Just like the shadows of a ball still represent a ball, all gradations of a standard must represent the standard because, in essence, they are all a *shadow* of the standard.

Each level of a learning progression has a different verb (different shape). How does this analogy relate to learning progressions? A learning progression example would be equivalent to a ball that casts a shadow of different shapes—a square, then farther away a triangle, and then even farther away a rhombus. If the verb is continually changing, students may find it difficult to know how they are doing and are more likely to default to passive learning. These different verbs make it difficult for teachers and students to use it to evaluate. You may need to modify the scale and use a less-rigorous verb to scaffold students to higher levels of learning.

With this said, proficiency gradations of a standard (where the verb stays the same in each gradation) are essential because without them, it would be harder to identify growth and provide actionable feedback to students. In order to create effective proficiency gradations, we generally follow these three rules.

1. **Don't be negative:** Each gradation level should represent something a student can do. While a single gradation may outline a lower level of skill mastery, it still communicates what the student is able to do. If we use negative language, we end up creating a gradation based on the deficiency—and that doesn't help students.

2. **Don't use numbers:** Using numbers is a sure way to communicate that learning is achievement based, and using cutoffs or bands is arbitrary and can cause students to make many assumptions about learning. However, using qualifying language, such as *productively*, *consistently*, or *adequately*, invites both you and your students to discuss the evidence of learning.

3. **Don't change the verb:** As we stated earlier, verb consistency is essential for students to understand what is expected of them. If the verb is the same at each level of the gradation, then the student can more easily shift his or her focus on modifying the language to understand what you expect.

Figure 3.10 shows an example of a proficiency gradation that follows the three previously listed rules.

Social Studies Skill: Argumentation

Exceeds Grade-Level Standard (4)	Meets Standard (3)	Approaching Standard (2)	Still Developing Foundational Skills (1)
I consistently communicate insightful arguments that establish claims and use evidence, elevated and complex reasoning, and sophisticated language appropriate for the task.	I consistently communicate arguments that establish claims and use sufficient evidence, elevated and complex reasoning, and language that is appropriate for the task.	I communicate arguments that establish claims and use limited evidence, basic reasoning, and often use appropriate language for the task.	I attempt to communicate an argument without establishing a claim or using necessary support, accurate analysis, or appropriate language for the task.

Source: ©2019 by Mount Vernon High School Social Studies Team. Used with permission.

Figure 3.10: Social studies proficiency gradations following the three rules.

We invite you to try using these rules with a real-life standard shown in figure 3.11. Using the verb *walk*, fill in the rest of the gradation language.

Walking (Skill)

Exceeds Grade-Level Standard (4)	Meets Standard (3)	Approaching Standard (2)	Still Developing Foundational Skills (1)
What is *exceeds grade-level standard*?	The baby can walk with no outside support.	What is *approaching standard*?	What is *still developing foundational skills*?

Figure 3.11: Example real-life skill with proficiency gradations.

The resulting proficiency gradations may look similar to figure 3.12.

Walking (Skill)

Exceeds Grade-Level Standard (4)	Meets Standard (3)	Approaching Standard (2)	Still Developing Foundational Skills (1)
The baby can walk with no outside support across various terrain.	The baby can walk with no outside support.	The baby can walk with minimal outside support.	The baby can walk with intense outside support.

Figure 3.12: Potential proficiency gradations for the skill of walking.

Another reason for using proficiency gradations is that they are much more effective at promoting efficacy since they include a single expectation, not four different ones. With a single expectation, students can spend more time in inquiry and open dialogue about that single expectation. This sustained inquiry can help them explore their learning boundaries more effectively (Schoemaker, 2011).

Differentiate Between Recursive and Nonrecursive Criteria

Admittedly, people tend to think of content and skills as separate items. Emily Rinkema and Stan Williams (2019) tell us otherwise. Skills can't be "separated from the content used to do them" (Rinkema & Williams, 2019, p. 32). Content is the lifeblood that brings the skills to life.

Organize Curriculum Around Skills, Not Content

Content does not play a less critical role in learning than skills do; it just needs to be subordinate to skills in curriculum organization. For example, you can't play the piano unless you know the notes. But when a piano teacher judges a student, he or she judges the student's ability to play the piano. The notes, tempo, and rhythm are all components of playing the piano effectively. It is the same in the classroom. Teachers judge students on how well they write, and they justify their evaluation by referencing how grammar, vocabulary, and structure positively or negatively affect the judgment. We refer to this subordinate content as *success criteria* (Moss & Brookhart, 2009).

As stated earlier, we usually see two types of success criteria—(1) recursive and (2) non-recursive. *Recursive criteria* are content that aren't designated by a unit, or aren't specific to a context. Instead, this type of criteria is the same, regardless of the unit of study. We typically find this type of criteria in English, fine arts, social sciences, world languages, and some CTE courses, where enduring skills and criteria are the same in each unit. Figure 3.13 shows an example of recursive criteria for the skill of scientific modeling.

Science Skill: Modeling

Exceeds Grade-Level Standard (4)	Meets Standard (3)	Approaching Standard (2)	Still Developing Foundational Skills (1)
I can interpret or construct an effective model in an unfamiliar context using all relevant key features.	I can interpret or construct an effective model in a familiar context using all relevant key features.	I can interpret or construct a model in a familiar context with some key features.	I can interpret or construct a model in a familiar context with support.
Success Criteria: • Creates labels • Built to scale • Correct associated relationships • Moves flexibly • Can be tested • Fits predictions • Solves a problem			

Figure 3.13: Success criteria for the scientific modeling skill.

This recursive criteria include *labels*, *scale*, *testable*, *solves a problem*, among others. You can use these criteria to create models representing a cell or an atom in biology or in other processes, no matter the unit or content.

The other type of criteria is *nonrecursive criteria*. These are criteria that change based on the context or unit of study. Teachers typically use these types of criteria in mathematics, science, and business; one unit might have specific criteria while, in another, they are entirely different. If we want to make the criteria for figure 3.13 (page 35) nonrecursive, we would simply change *creates labels* to *creates labels for cell organelles*. Or change *correct associated relationships* to *correct associated relationships between cells and muscle tissues*.

One last point about criteria involves their effect on pedagogy. It's important to understand which type of criteria you are using, as it has implications on your assessment, instruction, and grading practices. In the case of recursive criteria, we can view recent evidence as more relevant because the student has grown in the skill using the same criteria from the beginning of the semester. In the case of nonrecursive criteria, more recent evidence is not as helpful since they are not necessarily representative of the same content.

You can use the "Course Description" reproducible (pages 38–41) to help in assembling a course with all the needed standards, skills, proficiency gradations, and criteria. This process takes time and should be done with care. In the end, it is this curricular hierarchy that acts as the "vertebrae" for effective teaching and learning.

Conclusion

Starting with enduring, transferable skills allows you to form gradations of proficiency more clearly aligned to success criteria. It is essential to remember how important this work is for student self-efficacy, as it allows them to see the criteria needed for success. When students can see which criteria are needed at a given moment to demonstrate proficiency in a skill, it helps them own their learning and see where they need to go to develop proficiency or master the standards.

Big-Impact Recommendations for Implementation

The following four considerations are essential for effective curriculum development and set the foundation for all other practices that follow, such as useful rubrics, student-centered assessments and instruction, and evidence-based grading.

Refer to the following guiding points as you reflect and act on the information in this chapter.

1. Review the curriculum with each teacher or team to ensure that it is organized as *skills first, content second*.
2. Ensure that the skills are, in fact, enduring, transferable skills. For more guidance on how to do this, see *Collaborative Common Assessments* (Erkens, 2016).

3. A suggested goal should be to have three to seven enduring skills per course and one to three standards per skill (Guskey, 2015).

4. Consistently revisit the questions, What skills do we want students to develop? and How well do students need to perform these skills?

As you work through these guidelines, please note this work fits nicely into PLCs and curriculum improvement cycles. We often see teams working each week to revisit and revise work to make sure they are measuring exactly what they want students to know and be able to do.

Course Description

School Name: _____

Class Name: _____

Course Description: _____

Standards and Learning Targets

Skill 1:	Skill 2:	Skill 3:
Standard 1:	Standard 1:	Standard 1:
Standard 2:	Standard 2:	Standard 2:
Standard 3:	Standard 3:	Standard 3:

Proficiency Scale

Use the codes 4, 3, 2, 1, M, I, and N to communicate student progress in each learning target.

4	3	2	1	M	I	N
Exceeds Grade-Level Standard	Meets Standard	Approaching Standard	Still Developing Foundational Skills	Missing Evidence (Can be made up)	Students Turned in Incomplete Evidence (Can be made up)	Missing Evidence (Cannot be made up)

Performance Assessments

Feedback on learning can be given through informal and formal assessments. This can occur through in-class work; formative events; and mid-unit, end-of-unit, mid-course, and end-of-course assessments.

Specific Course Activities

In order to make satisfactory progress toward course standards, students will need to:

Specific Course Topics of Study

Required Resources

Textbook or Ebook Title and Description:

Additional Resources:

Makeup Policy

Grade Determination

Sample Grade Determination: The semester letter grade will be informed by the student's learning proficiencies over the semester-long body of work with consideration to retained proficiencies and growth over time. Mastery of learning targets leads to mastery of course standards, which in turn, leads to course mastery.

Grading Policy

Important Note: If a student has missing evidence in the form of M (can be made up) in any amount, then he or she runs the risk of failing the course. In these cases, there may not be enough evidence to determine target proficiency nor a course grade.

Scaled Learning Targets

Students will be given feedback on their level of proficiency toward mastery in each learning target using the gradations below.

Skill 1:

Standard 1:			
Exceeds Grade-Level Standard (4)	Meets Standard (3)	Approaching Standard (2)	Still Developing Foundational Skills (1)
Standard 2:			
Exceeds Grade-Level Standard (4)	Meets Standard (3)	Approaching Standard (2)	Still Developing Foundational Skills (1)
Standard 3:			
Exceeds Grade-Level Standard (4)	Meets Standard (3)	Approaching Standard (2)	Still Developing Foundational Skills (1)

Skill 2:

Standard 1:			
Exceeds Grade-Level Standard (4)	Meets Standard (3)	Approaching Standard (2)	Still Developing Foundational Skills (1)
Standard 2:			
Exceeds Grade-Level Standard (4)	Meets Standard (3)	Approaching Standard (2)	Still Developing Foundational Skills (1)
Standard 3:			
Exceeds Grade-Level Standard (4)	Meets Standard (3)	Approaching Standard (2)	Still Developing Foundational Skills (1)

Skill 3:

Standard 1:			
Exceeds Grade-Level Standard (4)	Meets Standard (3)	Approaching Standard (2)	Still Developing Foundational Skills (1)
Standard 2:			
Exceeds Grade-Level Standard (4)	Meets Standard (3)	Approaching Standard (2)	Still Developing Foundational Skills (1)
Standard 3:			
Exceeds Grade-Level Standard (4)	Meets Standard (3)	Approaching Standard (2)	Still Developing Foundational Skills (1)

CHAPTER 4

Develop Student-Centered Rubrics

The point [of rubrics] is to have students drill down to the specific areas of strength and those areas needing improvement.

—Cassandra Erkens, Tom Schimmer, and Nicole Dimich Vagle

Rubrics are commonplace in classrooms. They outline expectations, list criteria, and provide feedback to students. The issue is that teachers typically use rubrics only to diagnose deficiencies or communicate a grade. But to create self-reliant learners with high levels of efficacy, we should aim to create rubrics that help students understand what they can do and how to move forward.

Student-centered rubrics are like regular rubrics but with a different structure and purpose. Through student-centered rubrics, students get guidance about what they are expected to do, but more important, they get guidance on how well they are doing it. You can use student-centered rubrics to develop self-appraisal ability, something crucial to efficacy development (Bandura, 1997). These rubrics are the primary way students interact with curricular expectations. More important, student-centered rubrics can help students self-monitor, self-evaluate, and explore their affective reactions to learning, all of which are essential to a heightened sense of personal efficacy (Bandura, 1997).

How to Create Student-Centered Rubrics

Student-centered rubrics give students the opportunity to navigate and manage their learning, and the ability to become highly aware of the realities of their learning. They also allow students to have valuable conversations about learning outcomes with their teachers, peers, and parents. These conversations naturally lead them to evaluate themselves and others more effectively and to develop self-confidence.

To build these rubrics, let's look at three components that all student-centered rubrics should have: proficiency gradations, success criteria, and reflective space to discuss performance.

1. **Proficiency gradations:** The scales are the proficiency gradations outlined in chapter 3 (page 23). There is a single skill, along with the four levels of mastery—exceeds standard, meets standard, approaching standard, and still developing foundational skills.

2. **Success criteria:** Align all the available criteria for the unit of study. These criteria are the content, support skills, and concepts that students need to understand and do to master the enduring skill.

3. **Reflective space to discuss performance:** Create reflective space for students to connect or evaluate their mastery level with the criteria. Suppose a student gets an *approaching standard* in a skill; you would want him or her to explore which criteria led to that ranking. The process of self-evaluating proficiency levels and criteria is an essential part of learning (Brown et al., 2014). This space can also include your feedback, which involves dialogue with students to validate or refute their thinking.

It is important to note that all parts of the rubric, not just the reflection aspect, contribute to making it student-centered. Proficiency gradations provide a measuring stick against which students can compare their work to the desired proficiency. The listed success criteria give students context for the scale. When combined with the reflective space, students can better determine how they are doing on any of the criteria and identify what they need to do in order to demonstrate proficiency. All these parts of the rubric aid students' self-evaluation skills and self-efficacy.

Figure 4.1 shows an example of a student-centered high school rubric from a music class that contains these three components—the proficiency scale, success criteria, and reflective space to discuss performance. You will notice the four levels of proficiency, the success criteria covered to help get students onto the scale (gradation), and the reflective space for students to self-appraise where they are at in relation to the desired proficiency level.

Exceeds Grade-Level Standard (4)	Meets Standard (3)	Approaching Standard (2)	Still Developing Foundational Skills (1)
I can consistently play prepared music accurately and musically beyond grade-level expectations.	I can consistently play prepared music accurately and musically.	I can sometimes play prepared music accurately and musically.	I can sometimes play prepared music with support.
Success Criteria		**Student Reflection**	**Teacher Feedback**
<ul><li>I can exhibit grade-level-appropriate intonation and tone quality.</li><li>I can exhibit grade-level-appropriate note accuracy.</li><li>I can exhibit grade-level-appropriate rhythmic accuracy.</li><li>I can exhibit grade-level-appropriate technique.</li><li>I can demonstrate grade-level-appropriate musicality.</li></ul>			

Source: ©2019 by Mount Vernon High School Music Team. Adapted with permission.

Figure 4.1: High school music rubric—instrumental proficiency.

Figure 4.2 shows a high school science rubric used for planning and conducting investigations. (Please note that the science rubric is using recursive criteria that is not content specific. This rubric can be used to plan an investigation with cell membrane transport in biology or cardiovascular health in anatomy.)

Exceeds Grade-Level Standard (4)	Meets Standard (3)	Approaching Standard (2)	Still Developing Foundational Skills (1)
I can plan and conduct an investigation independently while making suggestions for extensions.	I can plan and conduct an investigation independently.	I can plan and conduct an investigation with some success.	I can attempt to plan and conduct an investigation.
Success Criteria		**Student Reflection**	**Teacher Feedback**
<ul><li>I can use appropriate tools to conduct the investigation.</li><li>I can use a directional hypothesis.</li><li>I can conduct an investigation that is clear and easy to follow.</li><li>I can collect relevant data.</li><li>I can conduct a controlled experiment.</li><li>I can account for errors and investigate again if necessary.</li><li>I can use appropriate terms from the unit of study in my investigation.</li><li>I can use correct principles.</li><li>I can include concepts from other curricular areas.</li></ul>			

Source: ©2018 by Mount Vernon High School Science Team. Adapted with permission.

Figure 4.2: High school science rubric—planning and conducting investigations.

Figure 4.3 shows a middle school mathematics rubric used for a geometry unit. Notice the nonrecursive, content-specific criteria that help guide students into the proficiency gradations.

Standard 1A—I can create visual and symbolic representations.			
Exceeds Grade-Level Standard (4)	**Meets Standard (3)**	**Approaching Standard (2)**	**Still Developing Foundational Skills (1)**
I can create an accurate visual or symbolic representation in any given context in unfamiliar situations.	I can create an accurate visual or symbolic representation in any given context.	I can create an appropriate visual or symbolic representation.	I can attempt to create a visual or symbolic representation.
Success Criteria		**Student Reflection**	**Teacher Feedback**
<ul><li>I can classify angles, triangles, and different polygons.</li><li>I can use the polygon formula with multiple variables.</li><li>I can write equations involving triangle properties.</li><li>I can write equations involving parallel line properties.</li><li>I can create accurate representations with precision.</li></ul>			

Source: ©2019 by Kim Bjork. Adapted with permission.

Figure 4.3: Middle school mathematics rubric—angles.

Figure 4.4 is a political science rubric with recursive criteria used multiple times throughout the semester.

Exceeds Grade-Level Standard (4)	Meets Standard (3)	Approaching Standard (2)	Still Developing Foundational Skills (1)
I can effectively communicate in terms of the specific task, purpose, and audience using a sophisticated level of engagement, vocabulary, and voice in my written and oral communications.	I can effectively communicate in terms of the specific task, purpose, and audience in written and oral form.	I can communicate in terms of the specific task, purpose, or audience in written or oral form.	I can attempt to communicate in terms of the specific task, purpose, or audience in written or oral form with a prompt.
Success Criteria		**Student Reflection**	**Teacher Feedback**
<ul><li>I can create relevant questions.</li><li>I can make a relevant and appropriate claim.</li><li>I can support my claim with multiple pieces of evidence.</li><li>I can demonstrate mastery of the appropriate terminology from the unit of study.</li><li>I can communicate in a way that furthers the author's purpose.</li></ul>			

Source: ©2019 by Ed Timm. Adapted with permission.

Figure 4.4: High school political science rubric—purposeful communication.

Develop Student-Centered Rubrics

How to Use Student-Centered Rubrics

Now that we've explored the importance of student-centered rubrics and how to create them, let's take a look at how to use them. The following are comparisons between student-centered and traditional rubrics and considerations for how to use student-centered rubrics to promote self-reliance and efficacy.

- Student-centered rubrics are for conversation; traditional rubrics are primarily for evaluation.
- Student-centered rubrics allow students to give themselves feedback; traditional rubrics provide feedback to students.
- Student-centered rubrics appear throughout the learning process; traditional rubrics appear at the end of the learning process.

Student-Centered Rubrics Are for Conversation; Traditional Rubrics Are Primarily for Evaluation

Traditional rubrics that focus solely on evaluation communicate many incorrect mindsets about learning. First, they communicate that learning and performance have a desired state. Students using a traditional rubric, which tends to outline the exact steps or which parts they must use, may begin to think there are precise formulas to learning. This type of rubric creates an external dependency on the teacher and diminishes the importance of intrinsic motivation and self-reliance, and sometimes the only thing it measures is the students' ability to follow instructions.

Second, traditional evaluation-centered rubrics tend to diagnose deficiencies. The language in these rubrics emphasizes *can't* rather than *can*. Students receiving a score of less than mastery commonly find negative words focused on what their performance lacks. With these deficiencies in tow, teachers tend to move on to the next unit of study in order to stay on pace. Due to this perceived time crunch, teachers may not give students a chance to react to feedback and learn from their thinking.

Figure 4.5 (page 50) shows a traditional English language arts rubric that is not student-learning focused but rather teacher-evaluation focused.

	Meets Standard (3)	**Approaching Standard (2)**	**Still Developing Foundational Skills (1)**
Development	• Supports claim with clear reasons and relevant and sufficient evidence and explanations	• Inconsistently supports claim with clear reasons and relevant and sufficient evidence and explanations	• Supports claim using reasons, evidence, and explanations that are insufficient or irrelevant
Organization	• Effectively introduces the claim • Organizes reasons and evidence logically • Provides a concluding statement or section that supports the argument presented • All citations are formatted correctly	• Introduces the claim • Organizes reasons and evidence in a manner that may lack cohesion (ideas may be rambling or repetitive) • Provides a sense of closure • Most citations are formatted correctly	• Claim is missing or unclear • Has little or no evidence of purposeful organization • Lacks a sense of closure • Few citations are formatted correctly
Language and Conventions	• Demonstrates an exemplary command of standard English language conventions	• Demonstrates a command of standard English language conventions; errors do not interfere with understanding	• Demonstrates a weak command of standard English language conventions; errors interfere with understanding

Approaching W.6.4: Produce clear and coherent writing in which the development, organization, and style are appropriate to task, purpose, and audience.

Meets RI.6.1.2.3: Cite textual evidence to support analysis of the theme, central idea, or to support claims.

Meets L.6.3: Use knowledge of language and its conventions when writing.

Source for standards: National Governors Association Center for Best Practices (NGA) & Council of Chief State School Officers (CCSSO), 2010a.

Figure 4.5: Evaluation-focused English language arts rubric.

Instead, we should strive to use rubrics like the one in figure 4.6.

Exceeds Grade-Level Standard (4)	Meets Standard (3)	Approaching Standard (2)	Still Developing Foundational Skills (1)
I can write an essay with a clear, complex purpose and thorough, multifaceted supporting details, evidence, and explanation.	I can write an essay with a strong, clear purpose and relevant, sufficient supporting details, evidence, and explanation.	I can write an essay with a clear purpose and some supporting details and evidence.	I can write an essay with a purpose.
Success Criteria		**Student Reflection**	**Teacher Feedback**
<ul><li>I can provide thorough research.</li><li>I can cite complete works.</li><li>I can use proper American Psychological Association (APA) formatting.</li><li>I can write clear topic sentences.</li><li>I can write catchy introductions.</li><li>I can write a decisive conclusion.</li><li>I can use the peer-editing process.</li><li>I can use an organizer such as an outline.</li></ul>			

Source: ©2019 by Alissa Sabers. Adapted with permission.

Figure 4.6: Student-centered rubric for advanced composition—essay writing.

Using this kind of rubric allows you to communicate forward-facing action that promotes growth (toward proficiency) and learning before a final mark is placed in the gradebook.

Student-Centered Rubrics Allow Students to Give Themselves Feedback; Traditional Rubrics Provide Feedback to Students

The most powerful tool that we have as teachers to ensure learning is the student's thinking. When you work to create a safe environment for students to observe, evaluate, and expand their thoughts, it increases the likelihood that students find the lesson more relevant and personal. Rubrics are an excellent way to help students explore and value their thinking. Rubrics used in this way can activate a process of personal-thought deployment, where students provide themselves feedback. The teacher only guides students if their thinking is off the mark.

This is an important point, as the burden of feedback should be on the student and the responsibility of validation on the teacher (Wiliam, 2006). Students should review and evaluate their work as much as possible, forming insights about their development. The teacher then affirms the self-feedback to activate a heightened sense of self-trust in the student, something essential to becoming not only a well-rounded student, but also a mature adult (Bandura, 1997).

To use student-centered rubrics for student-generated feedback:

1. Teach a couple lessons highlighting some success criteria, and follow up with a short formative assessment with the rubric attached to it.//
2. Ask students to self-score themselves on the rubric and justify that score.
3. Have students trade rubrics with a partner and either validate or refute the rating with evidence.

Student-Centered Rubrics Appear Throughout the Learning Process; Traditional Rubrics Appear at the End of the Learning Process

Rubrics should be the beginning of a learning conversation, not the end of one. If you use rubrics to evaluate rather than communicate, you run the risk that the conversation remains retrospective (for example, *should have done this* or *could have done that*). If you use rubrics to invite conversations about future development, you promote inspired action that can lead to investment in future learning.

Further, when you use rubrics to initiate conversations, you can create valuable time for students to react to self-, peer-, and teacher feedback during the learning process. When students get to review and use rubrics during formative moments, they can preemptively evaluate their learning. If you only give students the rubric at the end of a learning cycle, students have little chance to react to feedback.

To help with your rubric work, you can use the "Blank Rubric" reproducible (page 54) to develop and record your rubrics. You can complete this document for each skill or standard and add corresponding success criteria.

Conclusion

When you use rubrics that contain the aspects we have outlined in this chapter, you can create more student-centered rubrics that give learners the time to have valuable conversations about their learning and then react to and learn from those conversations. We also discussed that student-centered rubrics allow learners the ability to self-assess and self-appraise—two key traits that promote self-efficacy. Therefore, we must create rubrics with deliberate intent and use them in a manner that supports self-directed conversations and student empowerment.

Develop Student-Centered Rubrics

Big-Impact Recommendations for Implementation

Only after curricular work has been completed, with accompanying proficiency gradations, should you create rubrics. Once again, we recommend that this work be completed in departmental or course-alike cooperative groups to strengthen rubric development.

Refer to the following guiding points and questions as you reflect on the information in this chapter.

1. Rubrics should invite conversations about learning.
   Key question—Do our rubrics allow for students' voices?

2. Rubrics should be used for self-appraisal more than teacher evaluation.
   Key question—How often do we provide students with the rubric before an assessment or task?

3. Rubrics should only have criteria for the desired mastery level.
   Key question—Do our rubrics have criteria for non-mastery levels?

Blank Rubric

Exceeds Grade-Level Standard (4)	Meets Standard (3)	Approaching Standard (2)	Still Developing Foundational Skills (1)

Success Criteria	Student Reflection • What do I need to do? • What support do I need to do it?	Teacher Feedback

CHAPTER 5

Use Assessment as a Process for Learning

I came to realize that instead of going through [a traditional assessment] process, I could go directly to the students' contexts and simply work to make connections between what I observed and the content I was charged to deliver.

—Christopher Emdin

Any teacher knows that assessment is a critical component of quality education. When used properly, they provide students with the opportunity to build self-evaluation skills and emotional resilience to critical feedback. However, it is still more common for teachers to use assessment solely to evaluate students. Whether it is because of time, efficiency, or status quo, we can often make assessment an isolated and singular event. If we do not pay careful attention, learning can end up feeling like a seesaw; students always moving from assessment to instruction and back again. This "seesawing" can make assessments less dependable in producing reliable evidence of a student's learning, as we may struggle to know whether the performance is a burst of brilliance or a brief demonstration of mastery.

Deploy assessments not as disconnected events, but as a process in which each assessment is connected. This assessment process involves exploration, demonstration, reflection, and deliberation by students—all critical skills for self-reliance and independent adulthood. This is a continuously interwoven process of instructional elements and assessment aspects.

When assessment events are interwoven with instruction and grading, the result is a continual process of performance and reflection. In other words, there is no bouncing back and forth between instruction and assessment; there is just learning.

The benefit of doing this is that all events are considered viable moments. When all events are considered feasible for development and evaluation, students have more learning autonomy. This happens because there are far more opportunities to think, perform, evaluate, and reflect.

Figure 5.1 shows how assessments can be interwoven into instruction to provide a continual process of performance and reflection for students.

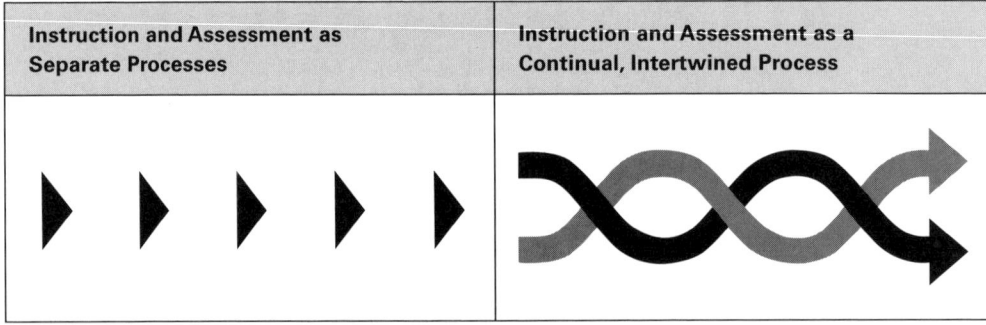

Figure 5.1: Assessment and instruction processes.

For assessments to be practical, they should be embedded into the learning process like the image on the right in figure 5.1. Do not relegate assessments to the end of the learning process; assessments need to happen in the moment, in and among instruction. When you do this, you and your students respond in real time to a student's performance; learning is authentic and feedback is instantaneous. You should aim to use a variety of methods to evaluate, analyze, instruct, and provide feedback, which makes the interaction between student and teacher far more relevant and meaningful. You and your students can use the "Planning Assessment and Instruction as a Continual Learning and Reflection Process" reproducible (page 62) to help design instruction that works as a continual process for learning and reflection.

How to Create Process-Based Assessments

Assessment is a perfect opportunity for students to use their thinking as a learning tool. With process-based assessments, students can validate and trust their thinking during the lesson. Once students build self-trust, they see their self-judgments as accurate and useful. Unfortunately, assessments are often mechanical and only reveal information that students acquire and memorize. Assessments should capture how students are thinking, not merely what they've learned. In order to promote assessments as a *process*, consider doing the following.

- Let standards guide assessment development.
- View assessments as experiences, not events.
- Use assessments to get to know students.
- Implement simulations, as they are crucial to learning.
- Make sure assessments are assumption proof.

Let Standards Guide Assessment Development

As stated earlier, powering, unpacking, and scaling essential learning standards is a critical practice for teachers. While these practices help you engage in critical conversations for curriculum development, they typically come from an incorrect view of the standards. This can have negative implications on how we build assessments. Teachers who define standards as only *what* they want students to know and do tend to build assessments by asking questions like, "What's the topic of the unit? How many questions are needed? What should the exam look like?"

We suggest letting the correct definition of a standard (outlined in chapter 3, page 23) guide assessment creation. Focusing on standard language helps you create assessments that are more authentic, reliable, and undoubtedly more meaningful to the student. When the language of a standard outlines how well a student needs to perform the skill or demonstrate the knowledge, teachers tend to ask the following question when creating assessments, "How much is enough of the right evidence, and how much is enough of the right evidence to accurately judge a student's proficiency?" *Enough* is when you have what you need to judge a standard accurately. *Right* tells you the right concoction of questions to elicit the information you need. You can use the "Gathering the Right Evidence" reproducible (page 63) to ensure you are gathering enough of the right evidence to assess students accurately.

View Assessments as Experiences, Not Events

When students engage with process-based assessments, they can view them as part of an ongoing story of learning rather than isolated incidents. Just like chapters in a book, one assessment should lead to the next, threaded together by skills, standards, and criteria.

Arranging assessments by skills, standards, and criteria gives you a way to get to know students and understand their ability levels. A simple way to thread assessments together through standards is to ask students before, during, and after assessments if they are ready to go on to the next question, section, or exam. Before answering, students take a few moments to reflect on what they have just done and how it might affect the next step in their learning. You don't need to use prompts on an assessment to put students in control of their learning stories; you can do this by taking time during instruction to ask questions such as, "How confident are you in your answer?" or "Before you go to the next question, is there anything you are still wondering about?" These types of questions help students see assessment as a process of learning and ultimately develop an internal locus of control that can yield insightful informations.

Use Assessments to Get to Know Students

We like to remind teachers there is no assessment police. No authority says you can't shape, mold, or change assessment to make student thinking more visible to help contextualize outcomes (Ritchhart, Church, & Morrison, 2011).

When we teach, we consider assessment to be a way to get to know our students, not to judge them. Process-based assessments can provide you the opportunity to *talk* with students about their learning and even gauge their social-emotional development. For example, instead of saying, "You need to include more relevant and accurate vocabulary in your essay—you earned four out of ten points," you can ask, "If you added [this word] or [this word], do you think that would add some clarity? If not, what words might you suggest?" By framing questions in this way, you give students the space to share their thinking, and you can gain insights into their entire learning profile, which is not visible in right or wrong answers.

Another example of using assessments to get to know students is by asking students to state whether they guessed an answer or were unsure after answering a question. What may seem confident reasoning may turn out to be guesswork. This type of process not only helps students qualify their responses but helps you understand the reality of a student's capabilities.

Implement Simulations, as They Are Crucial to Learning

Implementing formative assessments that simulate summative assessments helps create a more process-based assessment portfolio. Simulations are an excellent way to assess student proficiency while providing a safe environment for students to test their skill level. They also help students get a sense of the intended mastery of each skill and try it out before they are evaluated on it. To highlight this point, let's use a sports analogy. When we coach sports, we try to put the actual game back into a practice setting as much as possible. We wanted to know (as close as possible) how players might do in a real upcoming game. We would put players in situations that simulated the game. We would script out scenarios, trying to expose players to anything that might occur during a game. When coaches engage players in game simulations, players have a chance to visualize their performance and better adapt when they are actually performing. The same could be said for directors and actors during a dress rehearsal or for musicians during practice before performing a concert for an audience.

Perhaps more important, by putting a mastery experience into the practice setting, students have permission to fail without much consequence. With simulations, you can more appropriately react to resulting information and adjust instruction, so you know if students are ready for game day.

To find or create effective simulations, you should start by inventorying all the events in the unit, or course, to decide whether you can use them in a simulation. Consider the following criteria when determining if a simulation can be an effective assessment.

- It mimics the summative proficiency event.
- It can be marked without being graded.
- It allows students to experience and explore their learning.
- It is used to promote self-awareness, self-reflection, and self-appraisal skills.
- It is used in ways that are low or no stakes. Think of a dress rehearsal for a play. It simulates the play, but there is no critical audience.

Teachers who we work with on assessment also continue to find these criteria useful in creating simulations that act as assessments.

Make Sure Assessments Are Assumption Proof

Mental models are the mental representation of knowledge or skills (Brown et al., 2014). Students don't always create effective mental models but still get the right answers. Process-based assessments help expose these models and allow you to scrutinize the context through which a student arrived at an answer, rather than making assumptions about student thinking. When asking questions like, "What are you noticing as you work through this problem?," you gain more insight into students' learning profiles. Exposing these profiles should be invaluable to a teacher who wants to make his or her assessments assumption proof.

Figure 5.2 shows an example of a teacher attempting to make his or her assessment assumption proof. Note the questions asked after problem 1: What is the first thing you looked at to begin solving this problem? and What in the equation led you to believe your chosen answer is correct? These questions provided the teacher better insight into student thinking and prevented him or her from assuming students knew how to solve a problem simply because the answer was correct.

Multiple Choice: Circle the letter of the correct answer. Show all work for credit.

1. Solve: $(x + 1)(2x - 5) = 0$

    A. $x = -1$ or $x = 5$

    B. $x = 1$ or $x = -5$

    C. $x = -1$ or $x = \frac{5}{2}$

    D. $x = 1$ or $x = -\frac{5}{2}$

    What is the first thing you looked at to begin solving this problem?

    What in the equation led you to believe your chosen answer is correct?

2. Solve: $x(x + 4) + 3 = 0$

    A. $x = -3$ or $x = -7$

    B. $x = 0$ or $x = -4$

    C. $x = -4$ or $x = 3$

    D. $x = -1$ or $x = -3$

    What is the first thing you looked at to begin solving this problem?

    What previous skills that you learned are you relying on to solve the problem?

Figure 5.2: Assumption-proof algebra assessment.

In 2018, we spoke with a teacher who decided not to grade a project that she typically had graded in the past. She decided to use it only to gain insight into students' thinking and motivation. We asked her about the experience. She said students felt a sense of freedom to explore, experiment, learn, and reflect when the project was not graded but used for insight instead. She said the students were excited that they were not bound to the tension and pressure of getting a good grade. They took more ownership of their project and ended up presenting more in-depth knowledge than the teacher had received previously. This is not an isolated success story. Over the years, we have encountered many teachers who voiced the same feedback after they, too, used assessment more as a *formative friend* instead of as a *summative judge*.

Conclusion

Assessments should first and foremost build personal efficacy, which means assessments should always measure and promote a student's capacity to grow in healthy ways. There are many ways to make sure this happens: guide assessment development with standards; view assessments as experiences, not events; use assessments to get to know students; implement simulations, as they are crucial to learning; and ensure assessments are assumption proof. Finally, assessments should highlight a process, not a product, and be inseparable from curriculum and instruction.

Big-Impact Recommendations for Implementation

After completing your rubrics, work on creating assessments that effectively measure how a student is doing in relation to the assessed skill or standard. Refer to the following guiding points and questions as you reflect on the information in this chapter.

1. Align assessments with standards.
   Key question—To what extent do our assessments produce reliable evidence of standards?

2. Be sure assessments do not end learning conversations; instead, they should continue them.
   Key question—Do we include conversations in our assessment process?

3. Use assessments to get to know students.
   Key question—Do our assessments make students' thinking as visible as it needs to be?

4. Provide simulations of summative assessments as much as possible.
   Key question—Do we include enough scrimmages before the game?

Planning Assessment and Instruction as a Continual Learning and Reflection Process

Activity or Task Name	Assessment Components	Instruction Components

Gathering the Right Evidence

Use this organizational chart to list all your assessments for a particular unit, skill, or standard. After listing the assessments, it is easy to see if you have *enough* of the *right evidence*. Conduct three to five determining assessments so you have enough evidence to judge a student at the end of the reporting period. This also allows you to determine if you have enough developing assessments to give you and your students formative data to guide instruction.

Do We Have Enough of the Right Evidence?

Unit, Skill, or Standard:

Deliver (Formative)	Develop (Formative or Summative)	Determine (Summative)
• Ungraded • Used to develop prerequisite skills, create knowledge experiences, and offer feedback • Low or no stakes	• May be graded • Used to determine proficiency, create mastery experiences, promote self- and teacher awareness, and offer reflection and feedback • Low or no stakes	• Graded • Used to determine proficiency, judge mastery experiences, and create perspective (both self and third party) • High stakes

Small Changes, Big Impact © 2020 Solution Tree Press • SolutionTree.com
Visit **go.SolutionTree.com/schoolimprovement** to download this free reproducible.

CHAPTER 6

Implement a Generative Learning Model of Instruction

Context [must be] infused into instruction.

—Christopher Emdin

Over the last century, a lot has changed in education. We now have robust technologies that can provide engaging, vivid experiences for students as well as expanded research on the science of teaching and learning. Even with all these changes, the framework for building lesson plans and delivering instruction has not evolved much. Many teachers are still designing instruction around standards for the average-performing student, still structuring lessons in linear segments, and not embedding assessment into the lessons. When teachers use this type of instruction, they inadvertently create passive student learning (Emdin, 2016), failure deprivation (Hibbs & Rostain, 2019), and illusions of fluency (Schoemaker, 2011). These outcomes do not lead to self-efficacy and self-reliance.

Characteristics of a Generative Learning Model

Ideally, instruction should help students *generate* their learning, embrace and recover from their mistakes, and learn to react productively to feedback. Generative instruction is dynamic, malleable, and reactive to students' learning needs, and aligned to the true nature of learning.

To help you visualize what this reimagination might look like, let's use an eye exam analogy. When eye doctors examine patients' eyes, they do not predetermine which lenses to give them. They instead listen to their responses as they read each line of letters, change the lens, and then ask, "What do you see now?" Then the patient goes back and rereads the line.

If we extend this metaphor to the classroom, we would see a new instructional model emerge. We would see students produce evidence of learning before the teacher teaches. In a generative instructional model, students produce some sort of product (thinking or artifact) before the teaching occurs. In this way, teachers have a current state of learning to use *for* instruction.

In generative instruction, the student provides evidence, and the teacher adds context and nuance along with any new information. After this occurs, the teacher then directs the student to refine or reshape his or her learning.

Figure 6.1 shows an example of what generative instruction might look like for a lesson about writing an argument in elementary, middle, and secondary grades.

	Elementary	Middle School	Secondary School
Student Does First	To start the class, students circle a picture of their favorite season and write two words to describe the picture.	To start the class, students write a sentence or two about whether e-Learning or in-person learning is more effective.	To start the class, students write a few paragraphs to their parents stating why they should be able to stay out later.
Teacher Does Next	The teacher then instructs by putting a picture of each season on the projector and asks the students for their responses. The teacher writes the students' responses and then asks the students to choose two words to add to their paper.	The teacher then instructs on what makes a good argument while students review what they wrote. The teacher asks students what they might add to their sentences to make a stronger argument.	The teacher then instructs on what makes a good argument while students review what they wrote in their paragraphs to assess whether it was an effective argument.

Figure 6.1: Examples of generative instruction.

By instructing in this manner, you can help students become active agents of their learning, which leads to lasting proficiency instead of transient proficiency (Bandura, 1997).

How to Implement a Generative Model of Instruction

To do this, redesign instruction, making what is sequential and linear into something that is divergent, multifaceted, and reciprocal, and therefore generative. Generative models of instruction allow a student to "generate relationships and associations between stimuli and existing knowledge, beliefs, and experiences" (Hanke, 2012, p. 1356). The following are ways you can implement this practice.

- Design mastery experiences, not lessons.
- Align instruction to the true nature of learning.
- Use proficiency gradations during instruction.
- Leverage the inseparability of instruction and assessment.
- Use a diamond structure when lesson planning.
- Teach with student thinking.

Design Mastery Experiences, Not Lessons

As a classroom teacher, you learn quickly that learning happens less as a result of what you did to design a lesson and more from what the student realized during a mastery experience. Bandura (1997) points out, "[Mastery] experiences are the most influential source of [building] efficacy because they provide the most authentic evidence of whether one can muster whatever it takes to succeed" (p. 80). The effort put into creating perfectly formed lessons, while necessary, does little to drive learning (Schoemaker, 2011).

To design mastery experiences, include a mixture of the following formats: individuals, pairs or small groups, or large groups or whole class. Figure 6.2 (page 68) is what we call an *instructional diamond*. It is a planning tool to help teachers plan mastery experiences that start with individuals or small groups (small point of the diamond on the left), work to whole-class instruction (large middle section), and back out to individual work again (small point of the diamond on the right).

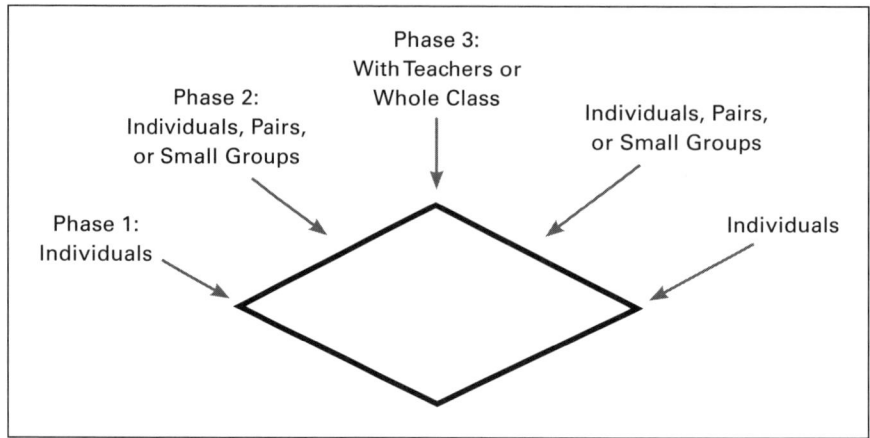

Source: Twadell, Onuscheck, Reibel, & Gobble, 2019.

Figure 6.2: Instructional diamond to help design a mastery experience.

To help you create this "diamond" lesson struction, consider the four following actions when designing mastery experiences.

1. **Personalize the learning:** Allow learners to privately scrutinize their state of proficiency and develop an awareness of their current state of learning or competence.

2. **Scrutinize the learning:** Allow learners to engage often in thoughtful dialogue with a variety of peers within multiple contexts (pairs and small groups) to examine their level of proficiency properly.

3. **Contextualize the learning:** Allow learners to gain an accurate perspective of their growth and abilities by hearing what you or the class has to say.

4. **Elaborate the learning:** Allow individuals and pairs or small groups to engage in individual adjustments or elaborations to their newly consolidated knowledge or skill. This practice is essential for helping students apply feedback, envision growth, and refine proficiency.

Figure 6.3 shows each segment of the instructional diamond and how the previously mentioned actions fit together.

Implement a Generative Learning Model of Instruction

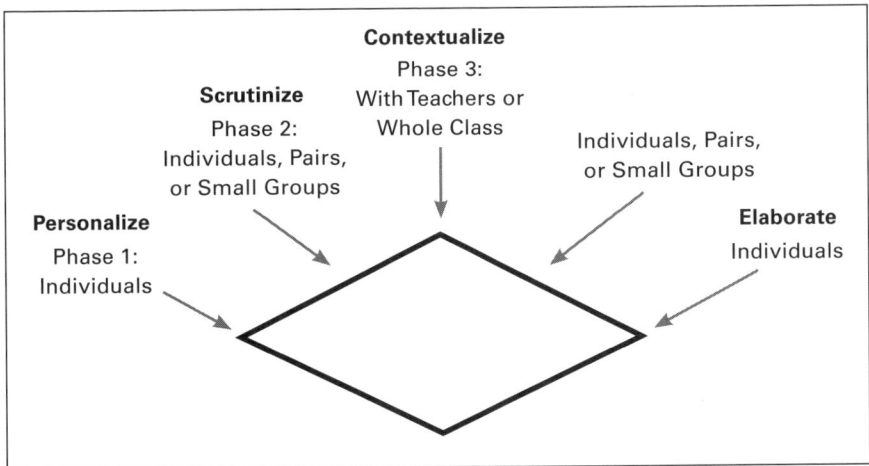

Source: Adapted from Twadell et al., 2019.

Figure 6.3: Another version of instructional diamond with actions built into the planning tool.

With mastery experiences, students have time to obtain a better sense of their learning, gain a more realistic perspective of self, enhance their self-appraisal skills, and self-sustain their learning.

Align Instruction to the True Nature of Learning

Many researchers (Brown et al., 2014; Carey, 2014) articulate that learning is a process of development and refinement, unsteady and fluctuating at first, but then, eventually, settling into a functional and rooted state (Jain & Reibel, 2018). Figure 6.4 represents this idea.

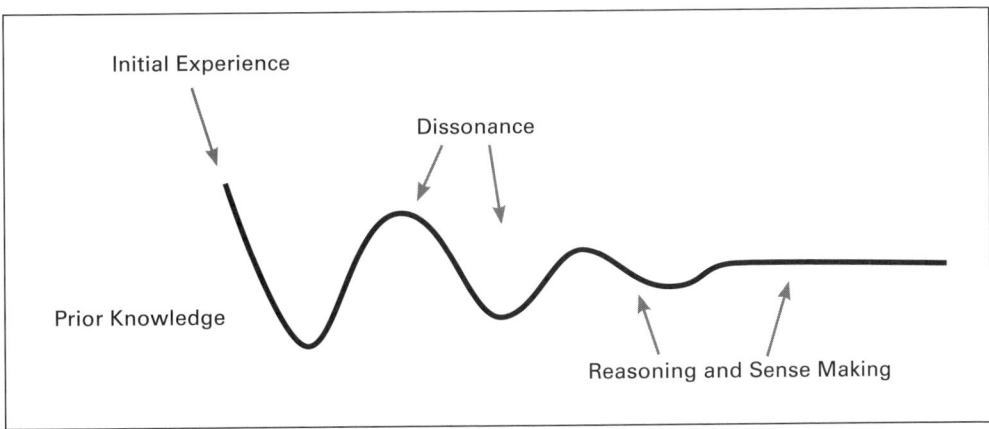

Figure 6.4: The learning process.

Experts such as Peter C. Brown, Henry L. Roediger III, and Mark A. McDaniel (2014) state that any new learning is labile, meaning while a student is learning, his or her knowledge and skills are malleable and easily altered. The diagram in figure 6.4 (page 69) represents this idea, and we hope that you consider referencing it when planning lessons.

To ensure that students cement new knowledge into long-term memory, build instruction around the *practice of failing*. When students experience failure safely during instruction, they improve their academic and emotional awareness. You are more effective if you allow students time for real-time reactions to their failures than if you cycle them through preplanned activities (Brown et al., 2014). When you help students learn how to fail first, you allow them the chance to build efficacy.

Use Proficiency Gradations During Instruction

By using a proficiency gradation during instruction, you know where to take the lesson *spontaneously*. This can work well after a formative check. Instruction expert Charlotte Danielson (2007) highlights this point when she writes that "teachers seize a major opportunity to enhance learning [when using proficiency gradations]. [They can] build on student interests or a spontaneous event or successfully adjust and differentiate instruction to address individual student misunderstandings" (p. 91).

The proficiency gradation acts as a map guiding the lesson. By using gradations, you can create lesson segments that are undefined, in which you can react to student needs and direct them toward proficiency in the moment. With students, you can mold the lesson while it is happening and sculpt the direction of learning based on student-produced evidence.

You can use the "Planning Instruction Using Proficiency Gradations" reproducible (page 77) to help plan proficiency gradations for your rubrics. The numbers represent the four proficiency levels. The descriptions next to the numbers outline the expected level of proficiency and how you measure said ability. Finally, the text in between the gradations represents the instruction that takes place based on student-produced evidence.

For example, if students produce evidence that fits proficiency level 3 (meets standard), you have already verified (assessed) student learning. You don't need an exam to prove this; you can immediately employ instructional strategies based on the evidence that can propel students to level 4 (exceeds grade-level standard).

Admittedly, adjusting instruction on the fly isn't always the easiest thing for a teacher to do, whether new to the profession or a veteran. If you add in all the things that can happen in the classroom, on top of possible negative behaviors and other student needs, this can be challenging. This takes time, but using proficiency gradations during instruction helps you to be prepared when these challenges arise.

Implement a Generative Learning Model of Instruction

Leverage the Inseparability of Instruction and Assessment

When you consider instruction and assessment as inseparable entities, classroom lessons can yield more, as they become primarily the acts of reflecting, relearning, and reapplying knowledge and skills. To help you visualize how you can make instruction and assessment more inseparable, we offer the following two examples: (1) assessment and instruction as separate, and (2) assessment and instruction as inseparable.

Assessment and Instruction as Separate

The following example shows how instruction is typically scaffolded (built on to the previous step) and demonstrates what we see in many traditional classrooms. The scaffolded instruction timeline follows this nine-step sequence.

1. Teach prerequisite skills and content.
2. Assess prerequisite skills and content.
3. Teach prerequisite skills and content.
4. Assess prerequisite skills and content.
5. Formally assess prerequisite skills and content.
6. Teach prerequisite skills and content.
7. Assign project combining prerequisite skills and content.
8. Provide summative experience to prove the cohesive application of prerequisite skills and content.
9. Conduct a reperformance of the assessment, if needed.

In this kind of instructional layout, teachers place the summative experience at the end of the learning cycle, leaving minimal time to reapply knowledge gained. Students don't own formative experiences. They simply take quizzes or do projects that the teacher evaluates. The supporting content is taught in a scaffolded and isolated manner, leaving students to think that these components may not relate to the unit standard.

Assessment and Instruction as Inseparable

The following example consists of six brief but complete instructional steps of prerequisite skills and content, an early summative experience, and then a cycle of formative performances and retakes.

1. Set expectations.
2. Teach prerequisite skills (success criteria and content).
3. Students initially perform.

4. Students evaluate and reflect on their performance.
5. Students refine their performance.
6. Repeat steps four and five as needed.

In this instructional model, not only are students practicing and learning, but they are aware of their learning, their growth, and the proficiency expectations. This awareness leads students to consolidate their learning faster and distinguish what their needs are.

Let's explore this idea further by extending this concept into a bike-riding metaphor.

Scenario 1: Assessment and Instruction as Separate
Standard: I can effectively ride a bike in a consistently safe manner.

Parents buy their child a bike. The parents sit down with the child at the kitchen table to teach him all the bike parts and their purposes, while the bike sits in the driveway. After several lessons, the parents ask the child to prove that he knows all the parts of the bike and how they work together. Once the child shows he knows the parts, the parents teach the child about bicycle rules of the road.

After several days, the parents ask the child to prove that he knows the bicycle rules of the road. Next, the parents ask the child to sit on the bike and recite each part and its purpose. Sadly, the child goes back inside the house to learn more about the parts and road rules to be sure he knows them. The next morning, the parents ask the child to take the bike apart and put the parts back together and maybe even paint the bike purple.

Finally, after many days, the child takes the bike for a spin for ten minutes. If the parents grade the child as unsuccessful, he is not allowed to try riding the bike again. The next day, the parents buy a boat and move on to teaching their child how to row a boat. If the child asks to ride the bike again before rowing the boat, the parents say, "Fine. However, you know doing this again doesn't teach accountability; you should have learned to ride the bike the first time."

This scenario is common in education today. Students are often taught about different content areas, but they are never given the chance to interact with the content in a formative and reflective way. When the time comes to be assessed, they either get it or don't get it, and everyone moves on, regardless of individual

Implement a Generative Learning Model of Instruction

student outcomes. However, when transferring this scenario to other areas of life, like riding a bike, it sounds ridiculous. Let's look at another scenario, which mirrors the logic model used in many areas of our lives, and we assert it should be used more often in education.

> **Scenario 2: Assessment and Instruction as Inseparable**
> **Standard: I can effectively ride a bike in a consistently safe manner.**
>
> Parents buy a bike for their child. They immediately take the child outside and ask her to ride the bike. The parents tell the child where to sit, place her feet, and grip the bars, but generally ask the child to start riding the bike. The child fails. When she fails, the parents ask her to ride the bike again, but this time, they intentionally modify support, change the context of feedback, and ask the child about the experience. In other words, the parents do not provide tips on what they saw, but instead, provide input based on what the child said about her own experience. After this exchange, the child rides again. The parents provide feedback based on the child's observation of the experience intentionally changing the path and pace, clarifying the purpose of the bike parts, and modifying support. The child rides again, this time, successfully!

In this scenario, the parents immediately put their child in a position for autonomous learning. They know that they can assess and instruct the child while she is riding the bike. The child rides the bike, and the parents observe, offer feedback, and differentiate their support. The child can trust feedback more because it is coming from her personal experience. This is also true in education. Providing a summative experience for students early and responding to student-produced evidence allows both you and your students to react accordingly and prescriptively to help students reach proficiency. By following these steps, students can fail but know that they can recover as you judge their work impartially.

Use a Diamond Structure When Lesson Planning

Let's go back to figure 6.3 (page 69). The left side (point of the diamond) represents individual work. As we move to the middle of the diamond (widest area), this represents whole-class or large-group instruction. Finally, as we move to the right point of the diamond, we work back out to small-group or individual work. The shape of the diamond represents the structure of the lesson, and the structure determines the purpose.

Teachers who use a diamond mindset when planning a lesson start with individual student work or small groups (left tip of the diamond) with some experience that exposes the students to the desired skill or proficiency. They can then combine small groups and move to broad group analysis and discussion (sizeable middle part of the diamond in figure 6.3, page 69). After the teacher finishes with whole-class instruction, he or she directs students to reflect on and perform pair or individual work (to the right tip of the diamond). Students react to the whole-class discussion by reengaging with peers or themselves. To create instructional diamonds, you can use the "Instructional Diamond Template" reproducible (page 78).

To demonstrate how to use this template to produce diamond lessons, let's look at the following example of a chemistry unit in which the teacher formatively assesses students on the skill of argumentation through the content of chemical and physical changes. The teacher uses the diamond template to start with individual work, moves into small groups, and then uses an example to address the whole class and give feedback. Lastly, the teacher asks students to perform changes based on teacher feedback to move toward proficiency.

Chemical Versus Physical Changes

1. Talk to a partner about the differences between chemical and physical changes, and support the differences with examples and evidence.

2. Mix-pair-share into thinking pairs. Compare your examples with one another. How can you incorporate new evidence into the argument? Make sure to challenge and critique each other with evidence.

3. Rotate to a different group, and compare reasoning with each other. Take time to revise.

4. The teacher takes one group's work and uses it to critique and engage the class. The feedback will be based on arguments with supporting evidence (skill language).

5. Small groups then make any needed changes (based on teacher feedback) at stations with a partner and write them down.

6. Students revise their claims and evidence individually and use the rubric to self-assess and obtain teacher feedback.

It's apparent that this teacher used very little direct instruction with students and let them do their thinking individually and in groups. The only teacher involvement was in the planning and group critique, in which he or she corrected and adjusted student thinking to the standard. Even after the critique, the teacher provided students with space to reflect, revise, and self-assess.

Teach With Student Thinking

This last point is an important one. We often tell teachers they should care less about what *they* think about student learning and more about what students themselves think about their learning. By helping students see their thinking as valuable, we empower them to take ownership of their learning as well as show respect for their individuality. When using student thinking to *grow students* (instead of *teacher thinking*), you help students become more self-reliant and confident learners. Danielson (2011) states that students should "monitor their own understanding, either on their own initiative or as a result of tasks set by the teacher" (p. 65). It is the "on their own initiative" part of this quote that you should strive for in your instruction.

Conclusion

Sometimes when a school is struggling with teaching, learning, and even culture, it often has to do with the lack of an instructional model. A clear instructional model can go a long way in providing all students with an equitable experience and make rigorous standards more viable. Taking the time to implement a "student-does-first" instructional model can make a big impact in a few ways; it can (1) illuminate student learning deficits before they become rooted, (2) provide more authentic feedback because the student had an experience before you started teaching, and (3) increase student engagement because they are now learning in a far more personalized manner. We hope this chapter provided clarity around a generative learning model and the instructional diamond to help you create more instructional cohesion in your school.

Big-Impact Recommendations for Implementation

So far, you have formed standards and worked on transferable skill development within your classes. You have developed student-centered rubrics you can use to interact with students regarding their proficiency expectations. You have started to develop the right assessment to determine student learning. As you think about these assessments and the instruction that is woven into them, look at putting mastery experiences back into the middle of the learning cycle. This initial step will give students the chance to better engage in the lessons and give you the chance to react appropriately to their learning.

We recommend bringing sample assessments and lessons to a department meeting for other teachers or team members to analyze. Ask critical questions, such as the following.

1. Does my assessment measure what it is supposed to measure?
2. How do I stretch my mastery experience back into the middle of the learning cycle?
3. How do I plan on using my rubrics or proficiency gradations during this process?
4. Are my lessons structured with the diamond template to maximize feedback and growth, and refine student proficiency?

Planning Instruction Using Proficiency Gradations

Exceeds Grade-Level Standard (4)
Meets Standard (3)
Approaching Standard (2)
Still Developing Foundational Skills (1)

Instructional Diamond Template

Use this template to create student-centered lesson plans in which each lesson starts with students performing, thinking, or doing. First, think about the standards you are teaching, which inform the lesson's purpose. Then, create lesson segments in the following order: (1) individual, (2) small group, (3) whole group, (4) small group again, and (5) individual activity as a conclusion. The last step would be to consider how much time each segment would take, which you record in the boxes on the left-hand side.

Time Allotted

☐	Individual Task or Activity
☐	Small-Group or Pair Task or Activity
☐	Whole-Class Task or Activity
☐	Small-Group or Pair Task or Activity
☐	Individual Task or Activity

CHAPTER 7

Provide Critical, Growth-Based Feedback

It's the doing something that defines effective feedback. If students aren't using it, teachers need to revise their approach.

—Tom Schimmer, Garnet Hillman, and Mandy Stalets

People's self-beliefs and actions can be affected (and even altered) by what someone tells them about their abilities (Bandura, 1997). Consider this point in the context of education. If we do not provide feedback with care, it can set in motion a downward course of mutual discouragement. As teachers, the most powerful tool we have to grow our students is our language.

To avoid this downward spiral, consider feedback as education's equivalent to customer service. When someone provides customer service to another, he or she empowers the customer to continue on toward his or her goal. This is the same concept for teachers. When providing feedback to students, we should strive to keep the responsibility of learning on them so they can continue toward their learning goals.

This is important because students typically try to keep the responsibility of their learning on the teacher. You may ask, "Isn't it the teacher's responsibility to get students to learn?" We propose that it is the teacher's responsibility *to help students learn how to teach themselves*—which is much easier said than done.

How to Provide Critical, Growth-Based Feedback to Students

Consider the following metaphor of tetherball. When two participants play tetherball, they hit the ball back and forth. Tetherball is similar to the game teachers and students play with learning. Teachers teach, students learn, students take tests, teachers grade and give feedback, and students ask for help. These actions go back and forth as students, perhaps unknowingly, try to keep the teacher responsible for most of their learning.

Good feedback is similar to a good game of tetherball. To play tetherball with your students, we suggest several ideas.

- Use rubrics to give prescriptive feedback, not diagnostic.
- Use summative experiences throughout a unit.
- Use rubrics to invite students into the feedback conversation.
- Use positive language on rubrics.
- Be positive, not punitive.
- Use nonevaluative language before evaluative language in feedback.

Use Rubrics to Give Prescriptive Feedback, Not Diagnostic

Think about feedback you gave your students recently or even feedback you received yourself. What did it say? How was it phrased? How did it make you feel? If it was positive, it was probably short with minimal information. If it was negative, it was probably diagnostic and focused on deficiencies. In our experience, teacher feedback follows this same pattern, typically stopping at diagnosis.

Diagnostic feedback tends to focus on the past and may lack the potential to lead to future action (Moss & Brookhart, 2012). Diagnostic feedback also tends to be deficiency focused, primarily for the sake of efficiency. It is more efficient and easier to notice something someone does wrong than what someone does right (Blanchard, Lacinak, Tompkins, & Ballard, 2002).

When teachers use feedback that is deficiency focused, it may come across as judgmental or pejorative, potentially leading to a lack of continued effort by students. This can prove to be especially problematic because if students do not *act* on teacher feedback, the words have little to no value. We encourage you to remember that it is the *resulting student action* that gives feedback its value, not its timeliness or its quality.

Provide Critical, Growth-Based Feedback

To get students to react appropriately to feedback, you should use more *prescriptive* (forward-facing) language. This kind of feedback includes phrases that offer a future course of action and describe the most likely trajectory of a student's learning. It is this forward-facing feedback that encourages students to take action—a small change that results in significant impact on student learning.

Figure 7.1 shows an example of prescriptive feedback. The far-right column shows prescriptive, growth-focused feedback. The columns leading up to that show how we got there. You can find a blank reproducible version of figure 7.1, "Changing Diagnostic Feedback to Prescriptive Feedback," on page 86.

Skill	Current Reality Feedback	Step 1: Depersonalize the Feedback	Step 2: Forward-Face the Feedback	Step 3: Invite Student Voice
Writing	You need to work on vocabulary.	Vocabulary is important for forming clear ideas.	The way you are using vocabulary will lead to forming clearer ideas.	The way you are using vocabulary will lead to forming clearer ideas. What other ways are you using vocabulary that will lead to a clearer message?

Figure 7.1: Example of changing diagnostic feedback to prescriptive feedback.

Use Summative Experiences Throughout a Unit

Another way you can create prescriptive feedback is to add summative experiences *throughout* a unit, not just at the end. Consider the following scenario: a teacher teaches a couple of lessons on content, engages students in activities, and gives formative feedback after a few quizzes. The teacher teaches a bit more, hands out a review packet, and provides a summative exam and a rubric with feedback. The problem with this scenario is the majority of the feedback only comes *after* the summative and formative assessments. Because of where it is situated, feedback is more likely to become diagnostic.

Instead, add summative simulations throughout a unit that are similar to the summative experience that ends a unit of study. This process allows you to more effectively provide prescriptive feedback and give students a chance to reflect on their mastery and make any necessary adjustments before the final summative assessment.

Use Rubrics to Invite Students Into the Feedback Conversation

During feedback moments, strive to use student thinking as feedback. It is important to remember that students do not grow from teacher thinking; they grow from *their own thinking* (Bandura, 1997). Encourage students to probe, prod, and be critical of their thoughts during the learning process—commonly referred to as *co-constructed feedback*.

When you provide co-constructed feedback, you encourage students to be the first to review their performance, the first to think about changes, and the first to remediate their work. All in all, teachers and students create co-constructed feedback together, making proactive and real-time decisions that can lead to more sustainable student development. Co-constructed feedback is best used *during* mastery experiences.

Let's revisit the Success Criteria section in figure 4.3 (page 47), as shown in figure 7.2. This rubric lends itself very well to co-constructed feedback, as students are the first to review their own work in the Student Reflection section. From there, you are better able to guide students toward proficiency with your comments. You can find a blank reproducible version of figure 7.2, "Success Criteria That Lends Itself to Co-Constructed Feedback," on page 87.

Success Criteria	Student Reflection	Teacher Feedback
• I can classify angles, triangles, and different polygons. • I can use the polygon formula with multiple variables. • I can write equations involving triangle properties. • I can write equations involving parallel line properties. • I can create accurate representations with precision.		

Source: ©2019 by Kim Bjork. Adapted with permission.

Figure 7.2: Success criteria that lends itself to co-constructed feedback.

Teachers who embrace a co-constructed response framework promote active student learning that can potentially lead to higher rates of feedback acceptance as well as higher levels of self-efficacy.

Use Positive Language on Rubrics

We will use a story to highlight the point of this section. In a discussion about feedback with Mount Vernon teachers, they asked us, "How do we give better feedback?" To this we replied, "Could you give student feedback without being negative?" In other words, could you interpret student work through the lens of what the student *can do* instead of what the student *can't do*? One teacher paused, thought for a moment, and then replied, "How are students going to know what they need to improve? I point out how they should address areas for growth. I am extremely detailed in what I tell them they need to work on, and I specifically communicate where they are lacking and tell them how to fix it." To this we added, "Although your feedback is prescriptive, you are starting from a place of deficiency when you first tell them where they are lacking. We are suggesting that you start from a place of proficiency and then prescribe how to improve." We then provided an example: "You could say something like, 'The way you wrote that sentence is clear for the reader. Now, what other vocabulary could you add to it to make it even clearer?'"

As we left, we worried, "Do other teachers feel the same way? Have we, the educational system, devalued the role of feedback so much that efficiency trumps sincerity?" Immediately, we felt we need to change the way we do feedback; it needs to be humanized—feedback that reflects kinship, care, and, above all, encouragement.

Be Positive, Not Punitive

When speaking of students at Stevenson High School, Ken Latka, dean of students at the school, says, "Be positive, not punitive" (K. Latka, personal communication, February 18, 2016). He uses this phrase to refer to student discipline, but this should also apply to feedback.

As teachers, we should use positive language to grow students. We should stop telling students about their *learning gaps* or *deficiencies*, and instead, notice what students do well, even the most minuscule demonstrations. In other words, catch them when they do something well, and encourage them to build on those competencies (Blanchard et al., 2002). Figure 7.3 (page 84) shows a few examples of punitive and positive feedback.

> **Punitive feedback:** "You need to add more details about cell organelles. It's not clear what you mean, and I am not sure if that is the correct detail to use there. This one detail is good, but the rest don't work."
>
> **Positive feedback:** "I like this one detail you added about cell organelles. Add in more of that to your work. You are on the right track if you keep adding in those types of details."

> **Punitive feedback:** "You do not engage in conversations effectively due to limited knowledge of the subject. You also should work on active listening skills."
>
> **Positive feedback:** "The more you listen and react to others' ideas using relevant facts and details, the better your engagement will be. If a classmate were to say _____ , what details from the reading could you add?"

> **Punitive feedback:** "You are missing basic details in the text. You need to read more closely."
>
> **Positive feedback:** "When you answered _____ , I could tell you were reading closely. Continue to do that on all questions, and I am confident you will comprehend more of the text."

Figure 7.3: Punitive and positive feedback.

Notice in the punitive examples, the teacher is specific but focuses on what the student *didn't do*. In the positive examples, the teacher focuses on what the student *can do*. Further, notice in the positive examples that the teacher points out any deficiencies through a positive perspective by stating what the student is able to do and giving let's-build-on-that feedback. For example, you might say, "Yes, what you did is a good start; now let's build on that to get you to [level of mastery]." Or even better, you could say, "Do you feel good about that [performance]? You should! What do you think you can do now as a result of that [performance]?" Although the former statement is positive feedback, the latter is positive feedback that builds personal efficacy.

Use Nonevaluative Language Before Evaluative Language in Feedback

In the classroom, try to have as many nonevaluative interactions with students as possible before evaluating them. Nonevaluative interactions encourage students to read the feedback, take it to heart, and apply it to construct further knowledge without the fear of being judged. During nonevaluative interactions, teachers tend to use more growth language, probing questions, and positively prescriptive comments that can help students see learning as a growth process. Without the fear of being judged, students are more likely to see potential in their learning, instead of defeat, as they realize it is possible to improve.

For nonevaluative interactions to be effective, resist the impulse to verify or classify student work too quickly; we call this practice *pausing evaluation*. Essentially, the idea of *pausing* is about teaching from *reflective* stances instead of *directive* stances. This means to pause evaluation, give students time to work and explore, and try to help them through critical curiosity and propelling questions.

For this to happen, you must care less about what you think about a student's learning and more about what the student feels about his or her own learning (Gobble et al., 2016). Remember, the goal of pausing evaluation is for you not only to verify the learning but to hold students responsible for ascertaining their learning. Nonevaluative feedback helps you to remember to extract, challenge, scrutinize, and contextualize evidence before ranking it.

Conclusion

Continually invest time in feedback. Students gain insights into their learning when you use positive, prescriptive, mutual, and nonevaluative feedback. Students can then use these insights to achieve a more accurate perspective of self, which will help them handle demands of cognition and their environment—demands that are inevitable in life.

Big-Impact Recommendations for Implementation

In chapter 4 (page 43), we learned that rubrics are a tremendous tool and take time to develop. They should be well-thought-out and intentional to allow co-constructed conversations centered on student-produced evidence. Rubrics are essential tools for learning, reflection, and feedback.

To help get started with providing positive, prescriptive, mutual, and nonevauative feedback, we recommend bringing a piece of evidence from a student and the corresponding rubric to a department meeting and asking colleagues the following three questions.

1. What would prescriptive feedback look like for this student? Does it lend itself to a future course of action that promotes student growth?

2. Which parts of the student sample can we highlight as positive to encourage growth in areas that still need work?

3. How do we make sure the feedback is nonevaluative (if not summative) to avoid classifying students too early?

Changing Diagnostic Feedback to Prescriptive Feedback

Skill	Current Reality Feedback	Step 1: Depersonalize the Feedback	Step 2: Forward-Face the Feedback	Step 3: Invite Student Voice

Success Criteria That Lends Itself to Co-Constructed Feedback

Success Criteria	Student Reflection	Teacher Feedback

CHAPTER 8

Leverage Reflection and Reperformance

Providing time and space to invite self-assessment is investing in students' learning stories.

—Katie White

One of our biggest realizations over the years is that most learning occurs *after* student reflection. In his book *Brilliant Mistakes*, author Paul J. H. Schoemaker (2011) helps us see this point, as he invites teachers to create lessons that activate student learning through reflective thinking. While many teachers include reflective segments in their lessons, far too many times, we see lessons still developed around tasks or physical engagement instead of student reflection and cognitive engagement. For example, figure 8.1 (page 90) shows a side-by-side comparison of a lesson focused more on physical engagement (following steps, performing guided tasks) and a lesson focused more on cognitive engagement (independent problem solving, reflection, and reperformance).

Notice that the lesson focused on cognitive engagement elicits more dialogue between teacher and student (drawing out misconceptions and reflection) than the lesson focused on physical engagement. By focusing on students' cognitive engagement, you provide students with the opportunity to trust their own thinking.

Lesson Focused on Physical Engagement	Lesson Focused on Cognitive Engagement
The teacher gives students a packet of steps for solving a series of equations.	The teacher gives students equation 3 and the steps for solving it. Students complete the equation.
The teacher reviews each four-step process in the packet.	Students compare their equation 3 answers with a partner and make adjustments.
The teacher models how he or she would solve equation 3 and calls on students. Students solve the equation along with the teacher.	The teacher models how he or she would solve equation 3, answers students' questions, and shows misconceptions.
Students work on an activity in which they have to match a step of the process to an example.	Students complete equation 4 in pairs.
The teacher models how he or she would solve equation 4 and calls on students.	The teacher models how he or she would solve equation 4, answers students' questions, and shows misconceptions.
Students complete equation 4 in small groups. Equation 4 is formatted so students complete each step in order.	Students return to equation 4 and reflect on why they did or did not complete it correctly.
The teacher models how he or she would solve equation 5 and calls on students.	Students self-evaluate their level of proficiency in solving a series of equations.

Figure 8.1: Comparison of a lesson focused on physical engagement and a lesson focused on cognitive engagement.

For students to develop trust in their thinking, a foundational aspect of efficacy, plan lessons around reflective thought more than anything else. When the focus of a lesson is reflective thinking, students can become more highly aware of their current state of competence, their emotions, and how to better accept critical feedback—all of which help them develop much-needed learning stamina. Focusing on student reflection can also help you better observe, support, and inspire student learning, instead of being stuck in the modes of delivery, evaluation, and intervention.

How to Add More Student Reflection to Lessons

With all that said, adding more student reflection to lessons is easier said than done. However, we suggest adding the following elements to your lessons to better focus on student reflection.

- Serious self-questioning
- Self-deliberation
- Reliable reflective mechanics
- Differentiated reflection

Serious Self-Questioning

One of the most enduring concepts we have learned from experts Rick Stiggins, Judith Arter, Jan Chappuis, and Stephen Chappuis (2004) is the following set of scrutinizing student reflective questions.

- Where am I going?
- Where am I now?
- How can I close the gap?

Teachers have historically tried to use these questions to stimulate reflection; however, students have more commonly used them to identify deficiencies and focus on achievement. To that end, we offer the following questions that students can ask themselves to better promote reflection and metacognition.

- How well am I supposed to be doing? Am I where I am supposed to be?
- What is helping me be where I am supposed to be?
- What is preventing me from being where I am supposed to be?
- What thinking led me to where I currently am?
- Knowing this, how am I going to get from where I am now to where I need to be?

Since these questions are much more focused on self-appraisal and self-awareness than the previous questions, it is more likely that students will engage with the material in a reflective manner rather than a procedural manner.

Self-Deliberation

Self-deliberation is critical to the learning process. Even a slight distortion in perspective, overconfidence, or lack of certainty about where they stand can lead students to distrust the learning process. The more time students spend deliberating, the more they can understand the skills or knowledge they may be lacking, but more importantly, they can begin to trust their own thinking.

When you add in self-deliberation segments to lessons, you give students an extended opportunity to engage in reflective dialogue with a peer or independent thinking about their *learning*. These opportunities can provide students with the time for processing and, more important, the reapplication of feedback. Ultimately, it is through self-deliberation that students can gain perspectives about their learning that are authentic, reliable, and relevant.

Reliable Reflective Mechanics

For students to deliberate and self-question meaningfully, they need first to know *how* to do so. You can build a student's reflective mechanics by deploying different types of reflective experiences in which students engage. For example, if you want to promote skill reflection, you could build a lesson segment around the student question, What were the results of the approach I used—was it efficient, or could I have eliminated or reorganized steps? Or if you want to develop a student's ability to reflect on success criteria, you could include a learning experience around the question, Did my response completely cover all parts of the assignment? The following list offers some reflective experiences, and associated student reflection questions, that our teachers have found helpful in developing student reflective mechanics.

- **Criteria reflection experience:** Do I understand the parts of the assignment and how they connect? Did my response completely cover all parts of the assignment? Do I see where this fits in with what we are studying?

- **Connection reflection experience:** How was this assignment similar to other assignments (in this course or others)? Do I see connections in content, product, or process? Are there ways to adapt it to other assignments? Where could I use this (content, product, or process) in my life?

- **Skill reflection experience:** Were the strategies, skills, and procedures I used effective for this assignment? Do I see any patterns in how I approached my work—such as following an outline or keeping to deadlines? What were the results of the approach I used—was it efficient, or could I have eliminated or reorganized steps?

- **Purpose reflection experience:** What am I learning, and is it important? Did I do an adequate job of communicating my learning to others? What have I learned about my strengths and my areas in need of improvement? How am I progressing as a learner?

- **Personal reflection experience:** What suggestions from my teacher or my peers can I use to improve my learning? How can I adapt this content or skill to make a difference in my life?
- **Growth reflection experience:** How can I best use my strengths to improve? What steps should I take, or resources should I use, to meet my challenges?

By building reflective mechanics with these types of reflective questions, you can help a student become more self-reliant, more self-motivated, and a more self-reflective learner.

Differentiated Reflection

In the classroom, it is essential to differentiate instruction. Teachers engage students in various ways, ranging from whole-class discussions to individual interactions—all based on individual student needs. Although teachers typically consider individual student learning needs when planning their instruction, it is *less* common for teachers to do the same for reflection events. If we are confident that students learn in different ways, why would we not consider that students also reflect in different ways? This consideration is important because of something called the *Dunning-Kruger effect*.

David Dunning (2011) explains this concept as the *double burden of incompetence.* This means that "those who are incompetent, for lack of a better term, have little insight into their incompetence" (Dunning, 2011, p. 260). Essentially, he states that low performers also possess limited ability for reflection.

Justin Kruger and David Dunning (1999) conclude that on any given assessment, there are commonly high performers (competent students) and low performers (incompetent students). The high performers typically know why they might have performed poorly in certain areas, but the low performers typically do not have the slightest clue about why they performed poorly. This doesn't mean that high performers don't struggle with reflection. Kruger and Dunning (1999) find that high performers tend to feel more insecure about their performance, potentially overreacting to errors.

The graph in figure 8.2 (page 94) represents this concept. The black line represents a student's actual performance score, and the gray line represents a student's perceived performance score.

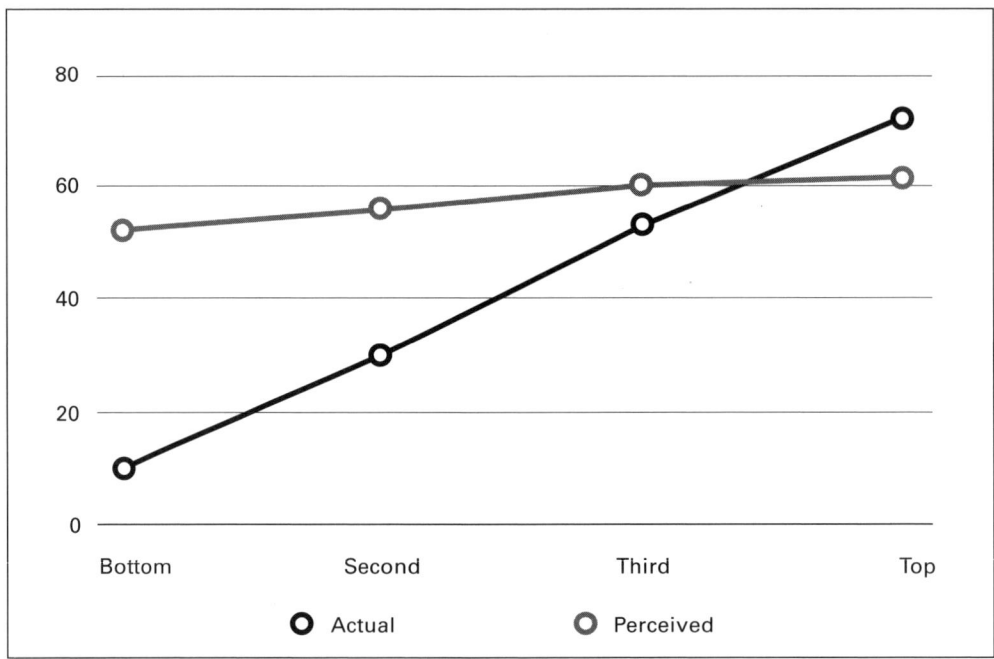

Source: Adapted from Kruger & Dunning, 1999.

Figure 8.2: Graph of student's actual performance versus perceived performance.

If bottom performers struggle with overconfidence and top performers struggle with insecurity, shouldn't we modify the reflective experience to meet the needs of these profiles? We say, yes! If we consider differentiated reflection as a valuable practice, we should be able to provide a more personalized and meaningful reflective experience to students.

Table 8.1 shows how each performance profile intersects with the Kruger and Dunning (1999) research and offers reflective questions and appropriate reflective activities.

By intentionally differentiating reflection, students can begin to more clearly see their competencies and gain confidence in those competencies. With the appropriate reflective activity, students can articulate much more clearly what is happening as they learn, which can lead to more proactive, prosocial behaviors in the classroom (Bandura, 1997). If we pay attention to these profiles when engaging our students in reflective experiences, we may be able to move student learning forward.

Leverage Reflection and Reperformance

Table 8.1: Reflective Practices for the Student Performance Profiles

Profile	Dunning-Kruger Effect	Key Reflective Question	Appropriate Reflective Activity
Bottom Performer	Overconfidence and misperception	What part of your answer makes you feel confident it is correct?	Guided individual contemplation and whole-class reflective activity for all students
Average Performer	Low self-appraisal skills	How would a classmate's answer compare to yours?	Peer reflection
Top Performer	False consensus and low confidence	How would you evaluate your results in comparison to class or historical data?	Individual item analysis

At Mount Vernon High School, teachers have commented about such reflective experiences, noting their students getting better at talking with each other about their development and evaluating each others' skills. In addition, teachers are noting students asking more questions about their own learning versus what they need to do to simply get an A.

Reperformance

It goes without saying that a student should be allowed to reperform after reflection. Not allowing students to perform work again, after they have had a chance to review what they originally did, is counterintuitive to the fact that feedback is provided for that very reason. Reperformances allow students another chance to demonstrate what they know and what they've learned *in response to feedback*. Since curriculum is focused on larger, transferable skills, it allows you to come back to the same skill at a later date and allow students to reperform work, maybe even with different content. To dive deeper into this idea, it is important to distinguish between the common practices of reassessments and reperformances.

Reassessments in Practice

According to common standards-based grading principles, reassessments are a way for students to redo or retry the same assessment (or one that is similar) for the sake of improving their score. For example, let's say a student just finished taking a test over the causes and effects of World War II. The student struggled a bit but earned a 2 on the proficiency scale as it relates to cause and effect. He would like to try it again after realizing what went wrong. If the teacher allowed a retry of the same or similar assessment, we would consider this a reassessment. (Note: We have seen some instances of teachers giving the same assessment, while others give an alternative version.) If the student improves on the retake, the new score should replace the old score, as it would be his most current state of proficiency.

While giving some form of reassessment or reperformance is the right thing to do, we've seen many teachers grow weary from allowing reassessment after reassessment. To that end, we believe the larger, transferable skills and standards work well for reperformances.

Reperformances in Practice

Three to five assessment events should give you enough of the right evidence to confidently judge a student in the transferable skills of a grading period. With that in mind, there isn't as much pressure to redo a particular assessment because you will most likely come back to assess that particular skill or standard a few more times during the grading period.

Let's return to the World War II assessment as an example, in which the student received a 2 on the causes and effects of the war. Instead of allowing a reassessment of the same test, you could wait until the next event, albeit with different content, to have the student demonstrate that he can in fact perform a cause-and-effect analysis. For example, the student may now be asked to apply that learning when returning to the cause-and-effect standard at a later date (this time, with the Vietnam War).

From a planning perspective, reperformances are essentially the next naturally occurring assessment of a transferable skill and standard, and can better provide students with more connected assessment experiences.

Conclusion

Students need space in order to develop and build trust in their own thinking. Be sure to provide time within your lessons for reflective thought, metacognition, and self-deliberation. Further, getting students to build reliable reflective mechanics by differentiating reflection for all learners helps students become more self-reliant, self-motivated, and self-reflective. After engaging in reflection, it goes without saying that students should be allowed a chance to reperform what they've learned.

Big-Impact Recommendations for Implementation

Admittedly, as you learn about reflection and reperformance and how to implement some of these strategies, a district could easily fill up a year's worth of professional development on the topic. Still, you can individually make small changes to have a big impact on reflection and reperformance in the classroom.

One form of easy implementation would be to try asking students the questions from the reflection list provided earlier in the chapter (see page 91), flipping the questions from a first-person perspective to a second-person perspective (adapted from Stiggins, 2006).

- Are you doing as well as you are supposed to be doing right now? Are you where I am asking you to be?
- What is helping you be where you are supposed to be?
- What is preventing you from being where you are supposed to be?
- What thinking led you to where you currently are?
- Knowing this, how are you going to get from where you are now to where you need to be?

When students ask themselves these types of questions, it makes learning more personal and generates more metacognition. This has a *big impact* on students' self-awareness and self-appraisal abilities as they take ownership of their learning.

CHAPTER 9

Use Evidence-Based Grading Practices

In essence, grading is an exercise in professional judgment on the part of the teachers.

—Thomas R. Guskey and Lee Ann Jung

Grading is one of the more familiar yet challenging aspects of a teacher's role. Ask any teacher, and one is bound to hear that the end of a grading period can be one of the most challenging times of the school year. Students may bombard teachers with questions about grade accuracy or even voice concerns about teachers' instruction and grading practices. These interactions can end with both teachers and students distracted from what is important—student learning.

We suggest reviewing students' evidence of competence to arrive at a letter grade, instead of point totals, averages, or other numerical grading policies. When giving grades, you should base them on each student's body of evidence of his or her proficiency in the course standards, not the student's ability to negotiate for more points or more opportunities. This practice is known as *evidence-based grading*.

Evidence-based grading is the collaborative process of collecting and interpreting student-produced evidence to provide students with an accurate perspective of their competence, interpersonal skills, and emotional resilience. Evidence-based grading is a type of competency-based grading that evaluates how well a student's current state of competence measures up to a standard of course skills. In our experience, evidence-based grading practices have had a positive impact on our school culture, teacher collaboration, and interpersonal relationships. In this chapter, we will explore how to implement this type of grading system.

How to Use Evidence for Determining Grades

In evidence-based grading, a teacher reviews a student's evidence—his or her body of work as well as recent evidence of competence in course skills. But this can prove tricky. To make the transition to this type of grading system easier, we have compiled a list of essential grading habits that can help you determine grades using an evidence-based process.

- Inform professional judgment with evidence.
- Align proficiency scores with letter grades.
- Include reperformances.
- Make the gradebook an active part of learning.
- Ensure there is enough of the right evidence.
- Assign incompletes as final grades, if needed.
- Communicate grades as trends and projections during learning.
- Assign grades *after* conversations with students.
- Consider homework as evidence.
- Rethink the format of culminating assessments.

Inform Professional Judgment With Evidence

We continue to hear that the traditional grading system is archaic. Traditional grading practices continue to enable students and parents to make assumptions about students' abilities (Guskey, 2015). Did the student get an A because he or she knew the material or had the skills down? Or is it because the student followed the teacher's model correctly? Or did he or she know how to "play the game" of school? You just can't be sure if you are *using points* to assign grades.

Evidence-based grading practices focus on student development and growth rather than on how quickly students learn or how many points it takes them to master a standard. Since teachers are focused on student development instead of points, they can provide more accurate insight into what students know and can do and their progress and growth over time.

Some critics point out that evidence-based models can be subjective and biased due to the fact that they rely on a teacher's professional judgment to assign a grade.

In our experience, we have found the opposite to be true. We contend that traditional grading practices are more subjective. Why is a question worth so many points? Why is one exam worth one hundred points, while the others are worth fifty points? Aren't the points awarded for participation and homework completion given for compliance?

We continue to find that with evidence-based grading, teachers are less subjective because the standards, scaled targets, success criteria, along with what proficiency looks like, are all vetted by a team of professionals. Grades are not determined by just one teacher's subjective view. This team effort allows for perspective calibration so teachers can make their professional interpretation of student learning. In sum, use your professional judgment when reviewing the overall body of evidence of work to determine a grade for a grading period.

Align Proficiency Scores With Letter Grades

You may be wondering if evidence-based grading still uses letter grades. Well, it depends on the school. If your school is like ours (Mount Vernon), which still requires letter grades on the transcript, the following offers an explanation for how traditional letter grades are determined in evidence-based grading.

> A+ = Highly refined competence in all skills
>
> A, A− = Competence in all skills
>
> B+, B, B−, C+, C, C− = Developing competence in all or certain skills
>
> D+, D, D−, F = No level of competence in certain skills (Lillydahl, 2015)

At the end of the semester, if evidence shows that a student is competent in all skills, then he or she should receive an A. Our suggested grade conversion, a "logic rule" that we use at both our high schools, is as follows.

> A—A score of 3 or 4 in each standard
>
> B—A score of 2 in any one standard (with grades of 3 or 4 in the remaining standards)
>
> C—A score of 2 in more than one standard (no score of 1)
>
> D—Any standard score of 1
>
> F—A score of 1 in more than one standard

Figure 9.1 (page 102) shows an example of a student's projected grade of A in Spanish. For this student, the standard scores (light gray bars) are all 4s, determining the student to be proficient, or projected to receive an A.

Evidence-Based Reporting		
▶ Biology S2		Projected grade: A
▼ Spanish 1 S2		Projected grade: A
Presentational Communication		4
1B Free write: Partner activity	02/05	3
1A Family project	03/21	3
1B Free write #5	03/21	4
HS.WL.02 – Interpersonal communication		4
2A Speaking activity	02/12	4
2A Movie conversation	03/06	3
2B Communication rubric	04/03	4
Interpretive Skills		4
3B Reading comprehension	02/01	4
Interpretive assignment	06/05	3
Culture		4
Cultural presentation #1	01/22	4
Cultural presentation #2	02/12	3
Guatemala free write	03/13	3

Figure 9.1: Sample evidence-based gradebook with projected letter grade.

Guskey (2015, 2020) advises teachers never to calculate academic performance, behavior performance, and development in the same grade, and we agree. Each area should get a separate mark or grade, with *academic performance* being the only category calculated in a letter grade.

Include Reperformances

A unique component in evidence-based grading is that students can have multiple opportunities to show proficiency in a standard before a grade is final. That said, not every assessment or task is available for a retake, and whether a student does do a reperformance depends on the teacher's discretion. Teachers may or may not require students to redo a task, assignment, or event; it depends on if they need more evidence.

In most instances, assessments (or tasks) work as a system, giving students several opportunities to show growth and improve their scores. If the assessments and tasks originally planned for a unit do not provide the teacher with enough evidence to judge students' proficiency, students can ask for a reperformance. Remember, the goal is student learning, not a chance for more points. Additionally, if a student can articulate how a reperformance aids his or her learning, this is a sign that learning is happening.

Further, you should consider reperformance scores in the final grade calculation. If a student reperforms and demonstrates a new level of proficiency, be it higher or lower, then you can consider the new score as part of the student's body of work.

Make the Gradebook an Active Part of Learning

Traditional gradebooks tend to function similar to bank vaults. Students check to see how many points they have earned or still need.

Since evidence-based gradebooks are organized by standards, events, and mastery scores, they act more like a book, where a student can connect past performances to current performances. When the gradebook tells stories, students can use it to guide any reflective conversations they may have with their teacher, as the information is organized in a more communicative manner.

A small, yet effective change is to use the gradebook *during instruction*, primarily during student reflection segments. For example, you may tell students to open up their gradebooks and then ask them the following questions as a bell ringer:

1. "In what standards would you say you are proficient? How do you know?"
2. "Are certain standards stronger than others? Why?"
3. "How would you predict your proficiency in each standard might change over the next few weeks?"
4. "How much confidence do you have in your proficiencies? If you don't have much confidence, how might I be able to support you?"

This small change can have a big impact on how teachers use the gradebook—as a *learning* tool, not just a *viewing* tool.

Ensure There Is Enough of the Right Evidence

Teachers often ask us, "How much evidence do I need to determine a grade?" To that, we say, "It depends on the nature of the skill." For example, when a teacher is assessing competency in writing, he or she may only need two pieces of evidence to determine if the student is a capable writer. Speaking, debate, or presentation may only require one demonstration to determine proficiency. Further, developing a reading competency may require many opportunities to determine if a student is a solid reader.

Figuring out how much evidence is needed typically takes determination, patience, and time. Although you should be diligent in maintaining records of evidence, we have found that teachers typically need about three to five pieces of evidence to accurately determine proficiency for a skill. If you do not get all the evidence that you deem essential, you should *not* determine a student's overall proficiency. It is your professional duty not to do so. In the case that teachers do not get *enough* of the *right* evidence to judge a student accurately, the grade of incomplete (events needed to determine a grade are not completed) or failure (evidence from events is academically unsound) is most appropriate.

Assign Incompletes as Final Grades, if Needed

Only consider proficiency in a standard if you have observed it as such *throughout* the semester. This is important because although a student may have some evidence of proficiency based on the small amount of work he or she did complete, it may not override the amount of missing evidence. It is important that you gather all the evidence you need and not trust a one-time burst of brilliance as reliable evidence. If you can't collect all the evidence needed to accurately determine a final grade, we suggest following these steps.

1. Change the grade to an incomplete.
2. Identify the standards that need more evidence.
3. Develop a plan with the student, which should consist of him or her completing any necessary assignments or assessments.
4. Communicate with the student to explain the consequences of not completing the missing work. For example, you can send a letter home to parents so everyone is on the same page regarding student performance. To help you communicate with students' parents, consider using the template in figure 9.2, which shows a sample letter our teachers send home to parents, using a made-up student name.
5. When complete, review the evidence with the student, and determine the appropriate final mark.

Use Evidence-Based Grading Practices

> Dear Parents,
>
> I am informing you that Jason is in my English class, and he is missing a vital piece of classroom work, a book report. I have already had this conversation with Jason as well but wanted to relay the same information home. With evidence-based grading, we need to see all significant pieces of evidence to accurately determine a final grade, including this missing piece of work. If we do not see this piece of evidence, it is difficult for me to assign a final grade, which may result in an incomplete (or possibly a failure for the course).
>
> If Jason is struggling with this particular skill or learning, please know I'm available to help before or after school. We also have a student services director who can help Jason.
>
> Thank you for your support. If there is anything I can do to help, please do not hesitate to ask.
>
> Sincerely,

Figure 9.2: Sample letter to send home to parents.

We have seen two things happen as a result of this practice: (1) the student works hard and demonstrates that he or she is proficient, or (2) the student still falls short of proficiency and realizes the original grade was correct. Either way, the final grade ends up being an accurate representation of the student's abilities.

Communicate Grades as Trends and Projections During Learning

Remember that you are the grade giver, not the gradebook. The gradebook should *suggest* a grade, not tell you what the grade should be. While some teachers continue to look at the entire body of work; others remain steadfast in their review of the most recent evidence, ignoring the earlier scores. In either respect, we suggest that you communicate grades as trends or projections.

For example, when parents take their baby to a doctor, the doctor weighs and measures the baby and then presents the results in terms of trajectories. The doctor outlines how the baby's current results foretell future weight or the growth trajectory for the baby's current height. This ongoing consideration of how the current body of evidence and recent scores predict future proficiencies is essential to conversations about student learning and assigning grades without surprises.

To communicate grades as trajectories, we suggest using two letter grades throughout the semester (not for final grades). For example, a student gradebook would show an A/B, B/A, C/B, or D/F, to name a few. This dual letter grade helps communicate that grades are projections and should not be the focus during learning; instead, it should represent learning, experience, and development.

Assign Grades *After* Conversations With Students

Further, it would be appropriate to invite students to review evidence from assessments and discuss the reasons why the student did or did not earn the final letter grade. Remember, evidence-based grading is about the co-construction of learning, which we should also apply to grading practices. To co-construct grades, you can converse with a student about the final grade using the evidence produced by the student. This practice can alleviate any tension or confusion that may exist between you and the student when awarding a grade because reliable evidence always shows the *why* behind the letter grade.

Consider Homework as Evidence

Homework remains one of the trickiest areas for successful implementation of evidence-based grading. It is easy to slip into the cyclical inquiry of *should homework count or not*? Students tend to react negatively to homework not counting in the grade because, traditionally, homework bolstered their grades by providing them fluff points.

In evidence-based grading, homework does not receive points, but instead *prepares* students for proficiency experiences. So, while it does not count in the way it did in a point-based system, it does still count. If students do not do the homework, there is a higher potential for them to receive a nonproficient score.

Instead of using homework to promote compliant behaviors, use lessons to create a *need* to do homework. This means creating learning experiences in which student performance depends on preparation. When students receive a nonproficient score, it should show that it was primarily due to not doing the homework. Students might then realize the connection between homework and proficiency. If they don't realize this connection and continue to not do the homework, this can be an indication of a more significant social or emotional issue.

Rethink the Format of Culminating Assessments

The traditional hour-and-a-half "pull it all together" final summative exam is not a practical aspect of evidence-based grading. In evidence-based grading, you should consider final exams not as a singular event, but rather as a process that takes place over several days or weeks. During this period, you can review evidence, talk with students, and allow them to reperform any standards in which they are still not proficient. Further, a process format allows for more student choice and voice, since students have more chances to provide you with evidence of their learning. Ultimately, this practice can lead to highly individualized and relevant culminating learning experiences for students.

Conclusion

Without a doubt, the more variables and factors included in a grade (besides achievement toward proficiency), the more unclear the grade becomes. It becomes like a giant breakfast burrito stuffed with all kinds of goodies, where you can't tell one ingredient from the next. It bears repeating that when you give grades, base them on each student's body of evidence of his or her proficiency in the course standards. When you do this, the gradebook becomes an active part of learning, clarifying to students, parents, and teachers exactly what the student knows in relation to the standard, thus, allowing you to make more informed decisions about your teaching and grading.

Big-Impact Recommendations for Implementation

Evidence-based grading practices are becoming more common as school districts look at fair and equitable ways to grade students. This chapter offered many small changes that can have big and lasting impacts. If school districts are looking to start small, they can begin by offering reperformances built into the curriculum or rethinking how to use homework. Going a step further, they can align proficiency scores to guide grades using the "logic rule" (see page 101).

Following are a few key points and questions to guide your work as you implement fair and equitable grading practices in your school and district.

1. Start by asking if your grading practices communicate exactly what you want them to communicate or if they include behaviors, formatives, and other factors.

2. Make sure to leverage reperformances throughout the learning cycle to give students the opportunity to improve their learning. Not all students learn at the same rate. Ask your team, "What is a simple way we can start to offer reperformances?"

3. Do you give final exams? If so, are they measuring what you want them to measure? Perhaps consider offering final exams as another opportunity for reperformance of a skill or standard.

4. Are you offering multiple pieces of evidence for each skill or standard? If not, consider how you can add enough pieces of evidence (three to five per skill or standard) so as not to measure a student on a fleeting moment of brilliance or failure.

5. Do your grading methods reflect a professional interpretation of evidence (body of work with consideration for growth)? Consider taking the most recent information into account regarding a skill or standard when assigning a grade.

CHAPTER 10

Establish Dynamic Reporting Structures

Do not let your decision to make grades reflect student achievement and support student learning and motivation depend on what report card format your district happens to use.

—Susan M. Brookhart

Reporting learning is almost as essential as teaching is in education. If we don't accurately communicate what students are learning, we may struggle to provide quality feedback, successful intervention, and final grades. Because of this, we suggest that gradebooks and report cards communicate *learning stories*. Each student is experiencing school internally, and externally, in uniquely personal ways (Kay, 2018), so why wouldn't gradebooks reflect each student's personal learning experience? In this chapter, we offer some suggestions that can lead to more informative and dynamic reporting structures in your gradebook.

Characteristics of a Dynamic Reporting Structure

In traditional teaching and learning, gradebooks are similar to bank vaults, as shown in figure 10.1 (page 110). Students earn points, the metaphorical gold coins. The teacher stores these gold coins, and at the end of the semester, he or she counts the gold coins and tells students their grades (based on their balance; Gobble, Onuscheck, Reibel, & Twadell, 2017).

04/30	Exam	Chapter 6 test	78/100	78	C+
04/26	Quiz #4	Graphing	40/50	80	B–
04/25	Practice Problems	p. 487: 11 and 33	0/2	0	F
04/23	Practice Problems	p. 463: 17–40	12/24	50	F
04/17	Practice Problems	p. 406: 25–30	4.5/6	75	C
04/11	Quiz #3	Trigonometry introduction	18.5/30	62	D+
04/09	Practice Problems	p. 430: 19 and 43	0/2	0	F
04/07	Practice Problems	p. 415: 13–28	12/16	75	C
04/05	Participation	Engagement in class	20/20	100	A
03/28	Quiz #2	Circumference	15/15	100	A
03/15	Quiz #1	Triangles	30/30	100	A

Figure 10.1: Traditional gradebook showing points and percentages.

While this practice is efficient, it can lead to assumptions about student learning and misperceptions of student ability. Further, gradebook software companies often create their products with a *bank vault mindset*, meaning that they create them to store points and show balances.

Instead, we suggest making your gradebook a library. Just like a library, it should communicate stories of learning, inspire conversations, and promote self-reflection. Ideal gradebooks convey a student's mastery of the essential and enduring skills for a class, provide useful feedback, highlight the trajectory of student learning, and ultimately are an *active part* of the learning process.

Figure 10.2 shows an evidence-based gradebook organized by course, by standard, by assessments, and by assignments, with the projected grade at the top right. Each light gray bar represents a skill or standard. All assignments that count toward the grade are below each light gray bar.

Establish Dynamic Reporting Structures

Evidence-Based Reporting		
▼ **Spanish 1 Semester 2**		**Projected grade: C**
Presentational Communication		3
1B Free write: Partner activity	02/05	3
1A Family project	03/21	3
1B Free write #5	03/21	2
HS.WL.02 – Interpersonal communication		2
2A Speaking activity	02/12	2
2A Movie conversation	03/06	4
2B Communication rubric	04/03	3
Interpretive Skills		3
3B Reading comprehension	02/01	3
Interpretive assignment	06/05	3
Culture		2
Cultural presentation #1	01/22	2
Cultural presentation #2	02/12	3
Guatemala free write	03/13	2

Figure 10.2: Sample evidence-based gradebook.

To communicate personal learning experiences, a gradebook should be organized into the following four sections (or *student stories*).

1. **How is the student growing?** The progress each student is making toward proficiency in each target and standard (not used to determine grades)

2. **How is the student performing?** Each student's current level of proficiency in each standard and target (used to determine grades)

3. **How is the student behaving?** Each student's effective or ineffective learning habits and behaviors (not used to determine grades)

4. **How is the student preparing?** A student's ability to build foundational skills and knowledge that precede the performance of standards and skills in the course (not used to determine grades)

We want to acknowledge that there are many different codes for reporting and communicating student learning; however, we have had success with the following codes.

How Is the Student Growing?

You can use the following codes to indicate any observed growth in a student.

- AG—Adequate growth
- MG—Minimal growth
- FG—Failure to grow
- I—Insufficient evidence

Note that these codes do not equate to a grade. You may use these codes to indicate if a student is growing at the rate you expect. For example, a student could have a C grade trajectory represented with an AG code. This example would indicate that a student is growing at the rate that you expect; however, his or her initial proficiency was low, as described in the following section.

How Is the Student Performing?

The answer to this question communicates information about the proficiency of each student. You can use the following codes to indicate the proficiency level of each student for course targets and standards.

- 4—Exceeds standard
- 3—Meets standard
- 2—Approaching standard
- 1—Still developing foundational skills
- M—Missing evidence; hasn't turned in yet
- N—Missing evidence; refusing to do
- ★—Anything marked with a ★ is not in the grade calculation

Establish Dynamic Reporting Structures

After seeing an evidence-based gradebook and its codes, some teachers might ask, "How should I handle missing work?" We suggest handling missing work or evidence as follows.

- Maintain specific deadlines.

- Each course sets its deadlines based on the nature of an event and the scope of the targets. Each course sets an X+ window to outline deadlines. X represents the actual due date, and + represents how many days a student has to make it up.

- An M represents missing work that the student hasn't done yet (within the X+ window). An I/A, I/B, I/C, or I/D displays as the projected grade until the work is turned in. The code of I represents incomplete. For example, I/A communicates that if the work is turned in, the student's final grade will be an A.

- An N represents missing work that the student is refusing to do (outside the X+ window). An I/F displays as the projected grade until the work is turned in. The code of I represents incomplete and F represents failing. The I/F communicates that if the work is not turned in, then the student's final course grade will either be an incomplete or a fail.

- If a student has any number of actual events that have Ms or Ns, he or she runs the risk of failing the course.

How Is the Student Behaving?

These gradebook entries show information about each student's work habits and behaviors, such as completing homework, participating in class, and staying on task. When you become concerned about one of these areas, you will enter one of the following codes.

- CN—Concerned about a student's behavior or social-emotional well-being

- Blank—A student's behavior or social-emotional well-being is as expected based on classroom norms and guidelines

- PS—A student's behavior or social-emotional well-being is *positively* influencing the culture of the classroom

Figure 10.3 (page 114) shows the student view of an evidence-based gradebook for a ninth grader, including behavior codes.

Semester 2					
Period Number	Course Name	Projected Grade	Weekly Academic Growth	Missing Evidence	Behavior Concerns
1	Study Hall				
2	Physical Education	P (Pass)	MG (Minimal Growth)		CN (Concerned)
3	Freshman English	C/D	AG (Adequate Growth)		
4	Algebra 1	A/B	MG (Minimal Growth)		PS (Prosocial Behavior)
5	Lunch				
6	Biology	I/A Incomplete (A if work is turned in)	AG (Adequate Growth)	Yes (Only Ms)	
7	World History	I/F Incomplete (F if work is not turned in)	FG (Failing to Grow)	Yes (Ns)	
8	Spanish 1	A/B	AG (Adequate Growth)		

Figure 10.3: Student view of evidence-based gradebook.

How Is the Student Preparing?

In evidence-based reporting, homework can be more than just assignments to take home and complete; it can serve several purposes.

- **Homework for instructional purposes:** In some cases, you may decide to give homework so students can prepare for the next day's lesson or to offer up opportunities for self-guided learning. In these cases, you *should not* enter the homework event in the gradebook.

Establish Dynamic Reporting Structures

- **Homework for completion:** If you are reviewing homework for completion only and *are not* checking it for quality, then codes that communicate submission status would be appropriate.
    - T—Turned in
    - TL—Turned in late
    - M—Missing
- **Homework for preparedness:** If checking for student preparedness, you should communicate how the homework or assignment demonstrates a student's preparedness for future assessments. In this case, you may use the following codes.
    - P (prepared)—Students have completed homework and nonevidential events in a manner that shows they are ready to now experience full mastery events, and there is a high likelihood of proficiency development.
    - PP (partially prepared)—Students have completed homework and nonevidential events in a manner that shows they are ready to experience full mastery events, but the likelihood of proficiency development is still low.
    - NP (not prepared)—Students have completed (or not completed) homework and nonevidential events in a manner that shows they are not ready to experience full proficiency events nor is there any likelihood of proficiency development.
    - M (missing)—Students have not completed the homework or nonevidential events.
- **Homework for evidence of proficiency and understanding:** You may choose to use homework as evidence of learning that factors into the grade. In this case, enter the homework in the academic standards section of the gradebook.

Figure 10.4 (page 116) shows an example of the homework section of an evidence-based gradebook. Notice that the teacher has chosen to use each homework assignment for a specific purpose—preparation, completion, and so on. You can find a blank reproducible version of figure 10.4, "Homework Log," on page 118.

Semester 1					
Category: Homework					
Name	**Due Date**	**Assigned Date**	**Score**	**Turned In**	**Comments**
Homework #1	08/24	08/22	T		Incomplete
Homework #2	09/02	08/29	PP	✓	Late
Homework #3	09/02	08/29	NP	✓	Late
Homework #4	10/16	09/13	TL		Incomplete
Homework #5	11/16	09/13	M		Incomplete
Homework #6	12/23	09/19	M		Incomplete

Figure 10.4: Evidence-based reporting—sample homework log.

Figure 10.5 helps summarize the codes previously discussed and how to record and report homework for an evidence-based course in the gradebook.

Using Homework for Preparation or Practice		Using Homework for Evidence of Proficiency	
For Completion	For Preparation	For Development (Inactive)	For Determination (Active)
T	P	4	4
TL	PP	3	3
M	NP	2	2
N	M	1	1
	N	M	M
		N	N
Enter codes in the homework or preparedness section of the gradebook.		Enter codes in the academic or standards section of the gradebook.	

Figure 10.5: Codes for entering homework in an evidence-based gradebook.

Conclusion

We suggest that you use dynamic reporting structures to communicate stories of learning and not merely the accumulation of points. You must tell the whole story: reporting out on growth, performance, behavior, and preparation separately from one another. When you do this, all stakeholders are able to clearly see how the student is performing in each area and make appropriate actions to improve.

Big-Impact Recommendations for Implementation

Over time, both Stevenson and Mount Vernon have developed add-ons to their online gradebooks to communicate what they would like to report regarding student learning. Gradebook add-ons are a small change with significant impact. However, before developing add-ons, schools may implement smaller changes that may or may not lead up to the bigger change, but are also very effective. Asking questions about grading is one of these small changes that can lead to a big impact.

As you look at your effective reporting procedures, ask, "Are teachers, students, and parents able to distinguish between how the student is *growing*, *performing*, *behaving*, and *preparing*?" If not, consider the following questions with teams, departments, or the entire staff.

- What should constitute a grade?
- Are there any ways we reward or punish students through our grading practices?
- Do our actions and reporting procedures match our beliefs about grading practices?
- Do our grades communicate to parents exactly what we believe constitutes a grade?
- What are some next steps we can take as individuals, departments, staff, or districts?

Asking these critical questions helps facilitate meaningful conversations and build consensus amongst the staff. Unity of voice becomes the needed synergy and momentum for change as educators take on dynamic reporting structures.

Homework Log

Semester:					
Category:					
Name	Due Date	Assigned Date	Score	Turned In	Comments

EPILOGUE

And now, the rest of the story . . .

We would like to take you back to the scene at the beginning of this book. We left off where Matt and his leadership team were dreaming about what it looked like to implement changes at Mount Vernon that might have a big impact on students—changes that were rooted in core beliefs and required minimal resources to implement because those changes resulted from habits of mind and commitments, not merely resources and systems.

When Matt and his team returned to Mount Vernon, they took some time to gather their thoughts on everything that took place at Stevenson. When team members came back together, they collectively decided it was time to take a further leap into school improvement. They determined their actions needed to match their beliefs about school reform. They needed to align teaching and grading practices and provide the structures to support such work. *In short, over a three-year period, Mount Vernon took on the very changes mentioned in this book and put them into practice.* Teachers and staff worked incredibly hard as they did this important work and built collective efficacy.

Admittedly, those were large reforms to take on in and of themselves; but, when broken down, each smaller change within each area of reform has had large impacts on self-efficacy and lifelong learning, for both teachers and students. The following are a few of the changes the team at Mount Vernon made and the potential impact they've had.

A New Focus on the Student

It was important to everyone at Mount Vernon to make sure the *why* was kept at the forefront of what they were doing. Initially, the *why* was about eliminating bad grading practices and moving toward evidence-based (standards-based) grading practices. The *why* was about eliminating extra credit, not counting homework in the gradebook, allowing retakes and reperformances, using multiple pieces of evidence, eliminating the zero, and so on—all sound standards-based grading practices. Although these are reasons that provide equity and justice to teaching and learning, what they didn't do was provide a compelling reason for change, one that left the team saying, "*This* is the type of student we want to produce when they leave Mount Vernon."

The team members dreamed of their *why* and what it would take for students to be college and career ready when they left Mount Vernon. These students needed to grow their self-efficacy, be complex communicators, and develop critical innovation and thinking skills. The team knew self-efficacy would provide students with confidence, reliance, and trust in their own thinking. It would allow them to see where they were at in relation to a teacher's, employer's, or someone else's expectations and have the confidence to know they could meet those expectations. They knew students who were complex communicators could communicate with others through a variety of means and platforms. They could not only communicate about what their grades are and why they got that grade (leading to self-reliance), but they could do it through a variety of platforms (such as written, oral, and technological).

The team knew critical innovation skills would prepare students to face many educational problems and life situations that would come their way. Students would possess skills that transferred not only from one class to another but from one life situation to another as well, best preparing students for success no matter what they did. The team believed its new *why* was exactly the type of student they wanted to see exit the doors at Mount Vernon.

Mission Statement Alignment

As the team moved forward, its work fit perfectly with its newly established mission statement, *Fostering growth and confidence as learners and people in society*. The work to be done would further the mission and vision and prepare students for their next step, whether it be moving to a new grade level, college, or the workforce. All arrows were pointing in the same direction.

Curriculum Review

During this process, it was essential to make sure teaching, learning, and reporting aligned with the why and the mission of the school. Teachers worked hard to create transferable skills and standards, along with accompanying proficiency gradations, to make sure learning goals were clear to everyone. The team formed rubrics along with success criteria to give students a clear picture of what it looks like to be proficient. Students noticed this change, as they have commented in open forums about how expectations were clear, and they knew exactly what they needed to do to be successful in their classes. Self-efficacy was definitely on the rise. Teachers also commented how this process made them a more effective teacher, while others mentioned having conversations around learning goals, which was different from conversations they had in the past.

Further, teachers tweaked and tailored assessments to align with standards and skills. Feedback from peers and teachers became a priority to move students from one proficiency gradation to the next, along with the opportunities for self-reflection. Daily lessons changed based on formative data collected and attention to the standard or skill being taught. For example, instead of asking students to list facts about WWII, teachers asked them to learn what happened in WWII and argue the causes and effects of the war *using facts.*

A New Look at Intervention

A new curriculum based on skills and standards has given even more purpose to a system of interventions. A universal lunchtime was created where students have a window of time to eat and then obtain any help they might need for any class. During this time, teachers extend and remediate learning as much as possible based on what students need. If more intense help is needed on a specific skill, teachers can "claim" students to make sure they gain valuable time to grow their learning in that particular area. In addition, a student support team was formed where students can be assigned to an actual class to get additional help in skill areas where they are deficient. Students are getting not only the help they need but the *right* help specific to their needs. A true system of supports has taken shape to support all learners at all times.

More Effective Collaboration Time

The team built PLC work time into the work day so teachers would have support throughout the day. Teams would now serve as the vehicle for moving teachers from where they were to where they needed to be. They would allow departmental teams to meet and provide support as critical curriculum work was to be done. Teachers would discuss essential skills to be learned, review rubrics and their intended use, align assessments, and calibrate scoring. They would fine-tune and adjust their unit plans to maximize use of their curriculum and instructional time.

Conclusion

All this work has taken time—as a matter of fact, it has taken more than three years. Along with time, it also has taken a collective commitment and a willingness to learn from others. It would be easy to say that 100 percent of the staff was on board and has loved every single change, but that would be a lie. This was not easy work, but it was the *right* work, and the team believed the benefits for students were worth all the hard work.

Without question, there have been hiccups along the way, and not everything has gone exactly according to plan. That being said, those are never reasons to hold back from what is best for students and preparing them for future success. Collective teacher efficacy doesn't require everyone to be on board. It might sound cliché to finish by saying that you never know the impact you might have with each small change you make; but *we do know the effects*. These are changes worth making.

We recommend using the ten recommendations outlined in this book as a buffet of small changes that can have a big impact. Without a doubt, we would recommend adopting all of them. However, starting with one or two feels manageable and ends up making the adoption of another one or two much easier. Take these ten recommendations to your team or department meetings, and ask which ones would have the biggest impact right away. These small changes can have a big impact on your school culture, your staff, and most important, student learning. We hope you find the courage to step up and make those small changes outlined in this book; and when you do, be prepared for the big impact that awaits.

REFERENCES AND RESOURCES

Adair-Hauck, B., Glisan, E. W., & Troyan, F. J. (2013). *Implementing integrated performance assessment.* Alexandria, VA: American Council on the Teaching of Foreign Languages.

Adams-Byers, J., Whitsell, S. S., & Moon, S. M. (2004). Gifted students' perceptions of the academic and social/emotional effects of homogeneous and heterogeneous grouping. *Gifted Child Quarterly, 48*(1), 7–20.

Ainsworth, L., & Viegut, D. (2006). *Common formative assessments: How to connect standards-based instruction and assessment.* Thousand Oaks, CA: Corwin Press.

Alhadabi, A., & Karpinski, A. C. (2020). Grit, self-efficacy, achievement orientation goals, and academic performance in university students. *International Journal of Adolescence and Youth, 25*(1), 519–535.

Amabile, T. M. (1983). *The social psychology of creativity.* New York: Springer-Verlag.

Artino, Jr., A. R. (2012). Academic self-efficacy: From educational theory to instructional practice. *Perspectives on Medical Education, 1,* 76–85.

Bandura, A. (1982). The self and mechanisms of agency. In J. Suls (Ed.), *Psychological perspectives on the self* (Vol. 1, pp. 3–39). Hillsdale, NJ: Erlbaum.

Bandura, A. (1986). The explanatory and predictive scope of self-efficacy theory. *Journal of Social and Clinical Psychology, 4*(3), 359–373.

Bandura, A. (1989). Regulation of cognitive processes through perceived self-efficacy. *Developmental Psychology, 25*(5), 729–735.

Bandura, A. (1997). *Self-efficacy: The exercise of control.* New York: Freeman.

Bandura, A. (2012). On the functional properties of perceived self-efficacy revisited. *Journal of Management, 38*(1), 9–44.

Bandura, A. (2018). Toward a psychology of human agency: Pathways and reflections. *Perspectives on Psychological Science, 13*(2), 130–136.

Bandura, A., & Wood, R. (1989). Effect of perceived controllability and performance standards on self-regulation of complex decision making. *Journal of Personality and Social Psychology, 56*(5), 805–814.

Barnes, M. (2015). *Assessment 3.0: Throw out your grade book and inspire learning.* Thousand Oaks, CA: Corwin Press.

Barton, A. C., Tan, E., & Rivet, A. (2008). Creating hybrid spaces for engaging school science among urban middle school girls. *American Educational Research Journal, 45*(1), 68–103.

Barton, L. G. (1994). *Quick flip questions for critical thinking.* Greenwood Village, CO: Edupress.

Black, P. J., & Wiliam, D. (1998). *Inside the black box: Raising standards through classroom assessment.* London: King's College London School of Education.

Blanchard, K., Lacinak, T., Tompkins, C., & Ballard, J. (2002). *Whale done! The power of positive relationships.* New York: Simon & Schuster.

Brimi, H. M. (2011). Reliability of grading high school work in English. *Practical Assessment, Research and Evaluation, 16*(17), 1–12.

Brookhart, S. M. (2017). *How to give effective feedback to your students* (2nd ed.). Alexandria, VA: Association for Supervision and Curriculum Development.

Brophy, J. (2008). Developing students' appreciation for what is taught in school. *Educational Psychologist, 43*(3), 132–141.

Brown, P. C., Roediger, H. L., & McDaniel, M. A. (2014). *Make it stick: The science of successful learning.* Cambridge, MA: Belknap Press of Harvard University Press.

Buehl, D. (2011). *Developing readers in the academic disciplines.* Newark, DE: International Reading Association.

Buffum, A., Mattos, M., & Weber, C. (2012). *Simplifying response to intervention: Four essential guiding principles.* Bloomington, IN: Solution Tree Press.

Burke, K. (1994). *The mindful school: How to assess authentic learning* (Rev. ed.). Arlington Heights, IL: IRI/SkyLight.

Cardwell, M. E. (2011). *Patterns of relationships between teacher engagement and student engagement* (Doctoral dissertation). St. John Fisher College, Rochester, NY.

Carey, B. (2014). *How we learn: The surprising truth about when, where, and why it happens.* New York: Random House.

Chappuis, J. (2009). *Seven strategies of assessment for learning.* Portland, OR: Educational Testing Service.

Collins, J. (2001). *Good to great: Why some companies make the leap . . . and others don't.* New York: HarperBusiness.

Csikszentmihalyi, M. (1990). *Flow: The psychology of optimal experience.* New York: Harper & Row.

Danielson, C. (2007). *Enhancing professional practice: A framework for teaching* (2nd ed.). Alexandria, VA: Association for Supervision and Curriculum Development.

Danielson, C. (2009). *Implementing the framework for teaching in enhancing professional practice.* Alexandria, VA: Association for Supervision and Curriculum Development.

Danielson, C. (2011). *The framework for teaching evaluation instrument.* Accessed at https://danielsongroup.org/downloads/2011-framework-teaching-evaluation-instrument on April 1, 2012.

Danielson Group. (n.d.). *A vision of excellence.* Accessed at https://danielsongroup.org/framework on January 8, 2020.

Dueck, M. (2014). *Grading smarter, not harder: Assessment strategies that motivate kids and help them learn.* Alexandria, VA: Association for Supervision and Curriculum Development.

Dunning, D. (2011). The Dunning–Kruger effect: On being ignorant of one's own ignorance. In J. M. Olson & M. P. Zanna (Eds.), *Advances in experimental social psychology* (Vol. 44, pp. 247–296). San Diego, CA: Academic Press.

Elbaum, D. (2015, May). The A.C.T. explorer reading model: Combining formative assessment and reading strategies. *The Assessor, 1,* 4.

Elder, D. (2012). *Standard-based teaching: A classroom guide.* Scotts Valley, CA: CreateSpace.

Emdin, C. (2016). *For white folks who teach in the hood . . . and the rest of y'all too: Reality pedagogy and urban education.* Boston: Beacon Press.

Erkens, C. (2016). *Collaborative common assessments: Teamwork. Instruction. Results.* Bloomington, IN: Solution Tree Press.

Erkens, C., Schimmer, T., & Vagle, N. D. (2018). *Instructional agility: Responding to assessment with real-time decisions.* Bloomington, IN: Solution Tree Press.

Faircloth, B. S. (2012). "Wearing a mask" vs. connecting identity with learning. *Contemporary Educational Psychology, 37*(3), 186–194.

Fast, L. A., Lewis, J. L., Bryant, M. J., Bocian, K. A., Cardullo, R. A., Rettig, M., & Hammond, K. A. (2010). Does math self-efficacy mediate the effect of the perceived classroom environment on standardized math test performance? *Journal of Educational Psychology, 102*(3), 729–740.

Flower, L. (1981). *Problem-solving strategies for writing.* New York: Harcourt Brace Jovanovich.

Flum, H., & Kaplan, A. (2012). Identity formation in educational settings: A contextualized view of theory and research in practice. *Contemporary Educational Psychology, 37*(3), 240–245.

Frey, N., Hattie, J., & Fisher, D. (2018). *Developing assessment-capable visible learners, grades K–12: Maximizing skill, will, and thrill.* Thousand Oaks, CA: Corwin Literacy.

Furrer, C., & Skinner, E. (2003). Sense of relatedness as a factor in children's academic engagement and performance. *Journal of Educational Psychology, 95*(1), 148–162.

Gates, H. L., & Steele, C. M. (2009). A conversation with Claude M. Steele: Stereotype threat and black achievement. *Du Bois Review: Social Science Research on Race, 6*(2), 251–271.

Gobble, T., Onuscheck, M., Reibel, A. R., & Twadell, E. (2016). *Proficiency-based assessment: Process, not product.* Bloomington, IN: Solution Tree Press.

Gobble, T., Onuscheck, M., Reibel, A. R., & Twadell, E. (2017). *Pathways to proficiency: Implementing evidence-based grading*. Bloomington, IN: Solution Tree Press.

Goddard, R. D., Hoy, W. K., & Woolfolk Hoy, A. (2000). Collective teacher efficacy: Its meaning, measure, and impact on student achievement. *American Educational Research Journal, 37*(2), 479–507.

Goddard, R. D., Sweetland, S. R., & Hoy, W. K. (2000). Academic emphasis of urban elementary schools and student achievement in reading and mathematics: A multilevel analysis. *Educational Administration Quarterly, 36*(5), 683–702.

Gonzalez, J. (2014). Know your terms: Anticipatory set. *Cult of Pedagogy.* Accessed at www.cultofpedagogy.com/anticipatory-set on November 25, 2019.

Graham, A., & Fitzgerald, R. (2010). Progressing children's participation: Exploring the potential of a dialogical turn. *Childhood, 17*(3), 343–359.

Gregory, K., Cameron, C., & Davies, A. (2011). *Self-assessment and goal setting* (2nd ed.). Bloomington, IN: Solution Tree Press.

Guo, K. (2015). What happens when students rent learning? *Statesman.* Accessed at www.statesmanshs.org/1055/features/what-happens-when-students-rent-learning on November 25, 2019.

Guskey, T. R. (2013). Special topic / The case against percentage grades. *Educational Leadership, 71*(1), 68–72.

Guskey, T. R. (2015). *On your mark: Challenging the conventions of grading and reporting*. Bloomington, IN: Solution Tree Press.

Guskey, T. R. (2020). *Get set, go: Creating successful grading and reporting systems*. Bloomington, IN: Solution Tree Press.

Guskey, T. R., & Bailey, J. M. (2001). *Developing grading and reporting systems for student learning*. Thousand Oaks, CA: Corwin Press.

Guskey, T. R., & Jung, L. (2013). *Answers to essential questions about standards, assessments, grading, and reporting*. Thousand Oaks, CA: Corwin Press.

Hanke, U. (2012). Generative learning. In N. M. Seel (Ed.), *Encyclopedia of the sciences of learning* (pp. 1356–1358). New York: Springer.

Hattie, J. (2012). *Visible learning for teachers: Maximizing impact on learning*. London: Routledge.

Hattie, J., & Yates, G. C. R. (2014). *Visible learning and the science of how we learn*. London: Routledge.

Heflebower, T., Hoegh, J. K., & Warrick, P. (2014). *A school leader's guide to standards-based grading*. Bloomington, IN: Marzano Resources.

Hibbs, B. J., & Rostain, A. (2019). *The stressed years of their lives: Helping your kid survive and thrive during their college years*. New York: St. Martin's Press.

Honicke, T., & Broadbent, J. (2016). The influence of academic self-efficacy on academic performance: A systematic review. *Educational Research Review, 17*, 63–84.

Jain, D., & Reibel, A. (2018, May). Creating competence in the classroom. *The Assessor.* Accessed at www.assessormag.com/uploads/2/1/9/6/21969098/assessor_edition_5.pdf on January 15, 2020.

Johnson, L. R., Johnson-Pynn, J. S., Drescher, C. F., Sackey, E., & Assenga, S. (2019). Predicting civic competencies among East African youth and emerging adults: Report on the Swahili General Self-Efficacy Scale. *Emerging Adulthood, 7*(4), 309–314.

Kay, M. R. (2018). *Not light, but fire: How to lead meaningful race conversations in the classroom.* Portland, ME: Stenhouse.

Kendall, J. S., & Marzano, R. J. (1997). *Content knowledge: A compendium of standards and benchmarks for K–12 education* (2nd ed.). Aurora, CO: McREL.

Ketelsen, T. (2017). *Student perspectives in advanced placement for first-year and traditionally underrepresented students: Successes, challenges, and shifts in their academic identity* (Doctoral dissertation). University of Portland, Oregon. Accessed at http://pilotscholars.up.edu/etd/26 on April 17, 2020.

Kohn, A. (2006). *The homework myth: Why our kids get too much of a bad thing.* Cambridge, MA: Da Capo Lifelong Books.

Kruger, J., & Dunning, D. (1999). Unskilled and unaware of it: How difficulties in recognizing one's own incompetence lead to inflated self-assessments. *Journal of Personality and Social Psychology, 77*(6), 1121–1134.

Lillydahl, D. (2015). *Don't touch my bucket of points!* Accessed at www.assessormag.com/dont-touch-my-bucket.html on January 15, 2020.

Lipton, L., & Wellman, B. (2011). *Groups at work: Strategies and structures for professional learning.* Charlotte, VT: MiraVia.

Maddux, J. E. (Ed.). (1995). *Self-efficacy, adaptation, and adjustment: Theory, research, and application.* New York: Springer.

Maddux, J. E., & Kleiman, E. M. (2016). Self-efficacy: A foundational concept for positive clinical psychology. In A. M. Wood & J. Johnson (Eds.), *The Wiley handbook of positive clinical psychology* (pp. 89–101). Chichester, West Sussex, UK: Wiley/Blackwell.

Maddux, J. E., & Stanley, M. A. (1986). Self-efficacy theory in contemporary psychology: An overview. *Journal of Social and Clinical Psychology, 4*(3), 249–255.

Marzano, R. J. (2003). *What works in schools: Translating research into action.* Alexandria, VA: Association for Supervision and Curriculum Development.

Marzano, R. J. (2006). *Classroom assessment and grading that work.* Alexandria, VA: Association for Supervision and Curriculum Development.

Marzano, R. J. (2009). *Designing and teaching learning goals and objectives.* Bloomington, IN: Marzano Resources.

McGuire, L., Mulvey, K. L., Goff, E., Irvin, M. J., Winterbottom, M., Fields, G. E., et al. (2020). STEM gender stereotypes from early childhood through adolescence at informal science centers. *Journal of Applied Developmental Psychology, 67,* 101–109.

McTighe, J., & Ferrara, S. (1998). *Assessing learning in the classroom.* Washington, DC: National Education Association.

Morgan, H. M. (2020). *Underdog entrepreneurs: A framework of success for marginalized and minority innovators.* Cham, Switzerland: Palgrave Macmillan.

Moss, C. M., & Brookhart, S. M. (2009). *Advancing formative assessment in every classroom: A guide for the instructional leader.* Alexandria, VA: Association for Supervision and Curriculum Development.

Moss, C. M., & Brookhart, S. M. (2012). *Learning targets: Helping students aim for understanding in today's lesson.* Alexandria, VA: Association for Supervision and Curriculum Development.

National Governors Association Center for Best Practices & Council of Chief State School Officers. (2010a). *Common Core State Standards for English language arts and literacy in history/social studies, science, and technical subjects.* Washington, DC: Authors. Accessed at www.corestandards.org/assets/CCSSI_ELA%20Standards.pdf on November 25, 2019.

National Governors Association Center for Best Practices & Council of Chief State School Officers. (2010b). *Common Core State Standards for mathematics.* Washington, DC: Authors. Accessed at www.corestandards.org/assets/CCSSI_Math%20Standards.pdf on November 25, 2019.

O'Connor, K. (2007). *A repair kit for grading: 15 fixes for broken grades.* Portland, OR: Educational Testing Service.

O'Connor, K. (2009). *How to grade for learning, K–12* (3rd ed.). Thousand Oaks, CA: Corwin Press.

Osborne, J. W., & Jones, B. D. (2011). Identification with academics and motivation to achieve in school: How the structure of the self influences academic outcomes. *Educational Psychology Review, 23*(1), 131–158.

Panadero, E., Jonsson, A., & Botella, J. (2017). Effects of self-assessment on self-regulated learning and self-efficacy: Four meta-analyses. *Educational Research Review, 22,* 74–98.

Pappas, C. (2014). *Instructional design models and theories: The generative learning theory.* Accessed at https://elearningindustry.com/generative-learning-theory on November 25, 2019.

Potts, G., Schultz, B., & Foust, J. (2004). The effect of freshmen cohort groups on academic performance and retention. *Journal of College Student Retention: Research, Theory & Practice, 5*(4), 385–395.

Reeves, D. (2006). *The learning leader: How to focus school improvement for better results.* Alexandria, VA: Association for Supervision and Curriculum Development.

Reeves, D. (2008). Leading to change / Effective grading practices. *Educational Leadership, 65*(5), 85–87.

Reeves, D. (2011). *Elements of grading: A guide to effective practice.* Bloomington, IN: Solution Tree Press.

Reibel, A. (2018a, May). Personal efficacy in education. *The Assessor, 5,* 19–20.

Reibel, A. (2018b, May). The three purposes of assessment: Deliver, develop, determine. *The Assessor, 5,* 14–15.

Renninger, K. A. (2009). Interest and identity development in instruction: An inductive model. *Educational Psychologist, 44*(2), 105–118.

Rinkema, E., & Williams, S. (2019). *The standards-based classroom: Make learning the goal.* Thousand Oaks, CA: Corwin Press.

Ripley, A. (2013). *The smartest kids in the world: And how they got that way.* New York: Simon & Schuster.

Ritchhart, R., Church, M., & Morrison, K. (2011). *Making thinking visible: How to promote engagement, understanding, and independence for all learners.* San Francisco: Jossey-Bass.

Rudasill, K. M., Capper, M. R., Foust, R. C., Callahan, C. M., & Albaugh, S. B. (2009). Grade and gender differences in gifted students' self-concepts. *Journal for the Education of the Gifted, 32*(3), 340–367.

Sandrock, P. (2011, December 8). *Designing backwards: From performance assessments to units of instruction.* Lecture conducted at the American Council on the Teaching of Foreign Languages, Lincolnshire, IL.

Savage, S. L. (2012). *The flaw of averages: Why we underestimate risk in the face of uncertainty.* Hoboken, NJ: Wiley & Sons.

Schimmer, T., Hillman, G., & Stalets, M. (2018). *Standards-based learning in action: Moving from theory to practice.* Bloomington, IN: Solution Tree Press.

Schoemaker, P. J. H. (2011). *Brilliant mistakes: Finding success on the far side of failure* [E-reader version]. Philadelphia: Wharton School Press.

Schunk, D. H., & DiBenedetto, M. K. (2016). Self-efficacy theory in education. In K. R. Wentzel & D. B. Miele (Eds.), *Handbook of motivation at school* (2nd ed., pp. 34–54). New York: Routledge.

Schwarzer, R. (Ed.). (2015). *Self-efficacy: Thought control of action.* London: Taylor & Francis.

Smith, R. (2017). Three aspects of epistemological agency: The socio-personal construction of work-learning. In M. Goller & S. Paloniemi (Eds.), *Agency at work: An agentic perspective on professional learning and development* (pp. 67–84). Cham, Switzerland: Springer International Publishing.

Sperling, D. (1993). What's worth an "A"? Setting standards together. *Educational Leadership, 50*(5), 73–75.

St.-Amand, J., Girard, S., & Smith, J. (2017). Sense of belonging at school: Defining attributes, determinants, and sustaining strategies. *IAFOR Journal of Education, 5*(2), 105–119.

Standard. (n.d.). *Merriam-Webster's online dictionary.* Accessed at www.merriam-webster.com/dictionary/standard on November 25, 2019.

Starch, D., & Elliott, E. C. (1912). Reliability of the grading of high-school work in English. *School Review, 20*(7), 442–457.

Stiggins, R. (2006). Assessment for learning: A key to motivation and achievement. *EDge, 2*(2), 3–19.

Stiggins, R., Arter, J. A., Chappuis, J., & Chappuis, S. (2004). *Classroom assessment for student learning: Doing it right—using it well.* Portland, OR: Assessment Training Institute.

Stiggins, R., & Chappuis, J. (2008). Enhancing student learning. *District Administration, 44*(1), 42–44.

Terada, Y. (2017). How metacognition boosts learning. *Edutopia.* Accessed at www.edutopia.org/article/how-metacognition-boosts-learning on November 25, 2019.

Toffler, A. (1970). *Future shock.* New York: Random House.

Tovani, C. (2012). Feedback is a two-way street. *Educational Leadership, 70*(1), 48–51.

Twadell, E., Onuscheck, M., Reibel, A. R., & Gobble, T. (2019). *Proficiency-based instruction: Rethinking lesson design and delivery.* Bloomington, IN: Solution Tree Press.

University of Illinois at Urbana–Champaign. (n.d.). *Illinois youth survey: Survey results.* Accessed at https://iys.cprd.illinois.edu/results on November 25, 2019.

Vatterott, C. (2009). *Rethinking homework: Best practices that support diverse needs.* Alexandria, VA: Association for Supervision and Curriculum Development.

Vatterott, C. (2015). *Rethinking grading: Meaningful assessment for standards-based learning.* Alexandria, VA: Association for Supervision and Curriculum Development.

Waack, S. (n.d.). *Hattie ranking: 252 influences and effect sizes related to student achievement.* Accessed at https://visible-learning.org/hattie-ranking-influences-effect-sizes-learning-achievement on November 25, 2019.

Wagner, T., & Dintersmith, T. (2015). *Most likely to succeed: Preparing our kids for the innovation era.* New York: Scribner.

White, K. (2017). *Softening the edges: Assessment practices that honor K–12 teachers and learners.* Bloomington, IN: Solution Tree Press.

Wiggins, G. (1996). Honesty and fairness: Toward better grading and reporting. In T. R. Guskey (Ed.), *Communicating student learning: The Association for Supervision and Curriculum Development yearbook* (pp. 141–176). Alexandria, VA: Association for Supervision and Curriculum Development.

Wiggins, G. (2010). Feedback: How learning occurs [Blog post]. *Authentic Education.* Accessed at www.authenticeducation.org/bigideas/article.lasso?artid=61 on November 25, 2019.

Wiggins, G., & McTighe, J. (2005). *Understanding by design* (2nd ed.). Alexandria, VA: Association for Supervision and Curriculum Development.

Wiggins, G. P., & McTighe, J. (2011). *The understanding by design guide to creating high-quality units*. Alexandria, VA: Associations for Supervision and Curriculum Development.

Wiliam, D. (2006). Formative assessment: Getting the focus right. *Educational Assessment, 11*(3–4), 283–289.

Wiliam, D. (2011). *Embedded formative assessment*. Bloomington, IN: Solution Tree Press.

Willis, S. (1993). Are letter grades obsolete? *Education Update, 35*(7), 4–8.

Winthrop, R., & McGivney, E. (2016). *Rethinking education in a changing world*. Accessed at www.brookings.edu/blog/education-plus-development/2016/09/12/rethinking-education-in-a-changing-world on December 29, 2017.

Woodcock, A., Hernandez, P. R., Estrada, M., & Schultz, P. W. (2012). The consequences of chronic stereotype threat: Domain disidentification and abandonment. *Journal of Personality and Social Psychology, 103*(4), 635–646.

Wormeli, R. (2014, November 12). *Standards-based assessment and grading*. Lecture conducted at the Illinois Association for Supervision and Curriculum Development's Curriculum 2020, DeKalb, IL.

Zimmerman, B. J., Bandura, A., & Martinez-Pons, M. (2011). Self-motivation for academic attainment: The role of self-efficacy beliefs and personal goal setting. In N. J. Salkin (Ed.), *SAGE directions in educational psychology*, (Vol. 1, pp. 231–242). London: SAGE.

Zimmerman, B. J., Schunk, D. H., & DiBenedetto, M. K. (2017). The role of self-efficacy and related beliefs in self-regulation of learning and performance. In A. J. Elliot, C. S. Dweck, & D. S. Yeager (Eds.), *Handbook of competence and motivation: Theory and application* (2nd ed., pp. 313–333). New York: Guilford Press.

INDEX

A

abilities, accurate perception of, 8, 10–11. *See also* self-appraisal; skills
academic acuity, 16
achievement. *See also* success
  self-efficacy and, 8
  success and, 14
Adlai E. Stevenson High School, Lincolnshire, Illinois, 1–2, 18, 83, 117, 119
agency, personal, 5, 13, 67
apathy, 8, 18
assessment, 55–63
  assumption proof, 57, 59–61
  creating process-based, 57–61
  culminating, 100, 106
  as experiences vs. events, 57, 58
  generative learning and, 76
  getting to know students with, 57, 58
  in the instruction process, 56
  leveraging the inseparability of instruction and, 67, 71–73
  recommendations for implementation, 61
  reperformance and, 95–96, 97
  rubrics and, 49–51
  simulations, 57, 59
  standards and, 57
assumptions. *See also* grading, evidence-based
  avoiding in assessments, 57, 59–61
  avoiding in mission statements, 18, 19–20

B

Bandura, A., 8, 10, 13, 17, 18, 67
bank vault mindset of grading, 109–110
behavior, reporting on student, 111, 113–114
belonging, 16–18. *See also* social connection

Brilliant Mistakes (Schoemaker), 89
Brookhart, S. M., 109
Brophy, J., 9
Brown, P. C., 70

C

career and technology education, proficiency gradation criteria for, 29
cast shadows, 32
challenges
  self-sustenance and, 9
  social connection and, 17
change, initiating lasting, 7
collaboration, time for, 121
Common Core State Standards for Mathematics, 24
communication. *See also* feedback
  about grades, 100, 104–105
  with parents, 104–105
  rubrics for conversation and, 49–51, 80, 82–83
  success and, 8, 11
community, 11, 20
competence
  differentiated reflection on, 91, 93–95
  rooted, 13
confidence
  reflection and, 96
  self-efficacy and, 8, 9, 18
content, skills vs., 23–41
control, 20
criteria. *See* success criteria
culture, 2, 75, 100, 113, 122
  mission statements and, 21, 22
curriculum, 23–41
  creating skills-based, 24–31
  enduring, transferable skills in, 24–25
  proficiency gradations vs. learning progressions and, 24, 31–34

proficiency gradations/scales and, 24, 26–34
recommendations for implementation, 36–37
recursive vs. nonrecursive criteria and, 24, 34–36
reviewing, 120–121
student engagement with, 9

D

Danielson, C., 70, 75
decision making, student-produced evidence for, 18, 20
deficiencies
　feedback and, 83–84
　rubrics in diagnosing, 49–50
Developing Assessment-Capable Visible Learners, Grades K–12 (Frey, Hattie, and Fisher), 13–14
diagnostic feedback, 80–81
differentiated reflection, 91, 93–95
Dintersmith, T., 7, 15
double burden of incompetence, 93–94
DuFour, R., 15
Dunning, D., 93, 94
Dunning-Kruger effect, 93–94

E

Emdin, C., 11, 55, 65
emotional awareness, 8, 11
　assessments and, 58
　mission statements and, 16, 17
empowerment, 22
engagement
　generative learning model and, 75
　physical, 89–90
　positive self-concept and, 9
　social connection, emotional awareness, and, 11
English language arts
　generative instruction in, 66
　prescriptive vs. diagnostic feedback in, 81
　proficiency scales for, 27
　rubrics for, 50–51
Erkens, C., 43
evaluation, pausing, 85
evaluative language, 80, 84–85
evidence
　grading based on, 99–107
　informing professional judgment with, 100–101
expectations, 43. *See also* rubrics, student-centered
experimentation
　assumption-proof assessment and, 61
　self-sustenance and, 9

F

failure
　accurate perception of abilities and, 10–11
　building instruction around the practice of failing, 70
　constructive, 12, 13–14
　positive vs. punitive feedback on, 80, 83–84
　productive vs. unproductive, 14
failure deprivation, 9, 65
Fast, L. A., 17
feedback, 43, 79–87. *See also* rubrics, student-centered
　co-constructed, 82–83
　generative learning and, 76
　nonevaluative vs. evaluative language in, 80, 84–85
　positive language in, 80, 83
　positive vs. punitive, 80, 83–84
　recommendations for implementing, 85
　reperformance and, 95–96, 97
　rubrics for, 49, 51–52, 82–83
　summative experiences, 80, 81
　tetherball metaphor of, 80
Fisher, D., 14
Fitzgerald, R., 10
Flum, H., 12
For White Folks Who Teach in the Hood . . . and the Rest of Y'all Too (Emdin), 11
Frey, N., 13–14

G

generative learning, 12, 13, 65–78
　aligning instruction for, 67, 69–70
　characteristics of, 65–67
　instruction implementation for, 67–75
　lesson planning for, 67, 73–75
　leveraging the inseparability of instruction and, 67, 71–73
　mastery experiences for, 67–69
　proficiency gradations and, 67, 70
　recommendations for implementing, 75–76
　teaching with student learning and, 67, 75
goals, self-sustenance and, 9
Goddard, R. D., 18
grading, evidence-based, 99–107
　adequate evidence for, 100, 104
　as an active part of learning, 100, 103, 110–112
　assigning after conversations with students, 100, 106
　bank vault mindset and, 109–110
　communicating trends/projections in, 100, 105
　culminating assessments in, 100, 106

gradebook organization for, 111–112
homework as evidence in, 100, 106, 111, 114–116
how to use, 100–106
incompletes and, 100, 104–105
logic rule for, 101, 107
professional judgment and, 100–101
proficiency scores and, 100, 101–102
recommendations for implementing, 107
reperformances in, 100, 102–103
reporting structures and, 109–112
Graham, A., 10
growth reflection experience, 93
Guskey, T. R., 27, 99, 102

H

Hammond, K. A., 17
Hattie, J., 13–14, 18
Hillman, G., 79
homework, 100, 106, 111, 114–116
Hoy, W. K., 18

I

identity
  accurate perception of abilities and, 10–11
  connecting learning with, 9
  intervention, support programs, and, 11
  mission statements and, 17
illusions of fluency, 65
incompetence, double burden of, 93–94
incomplete grades, 100, 104–105, 113
instructional diamond, 67–69, 73–75
interest, 16. *See also* identity; values
intervention, 11, 121

J

Jones, B. D., 16
Jung, L. A., 99

K

Kaplan, A., 12
Kruger, J., 93, 94

L

Latka, K., 83
learning
  articulation and communication about, 11
  assessment as a process for, 55–63
  avoiding assumptions about, 18, 19–20
  connecting with identity, 9
  contextualizing, 68–69
  defining, 12–14
  drive for, 8
  efficacious traits for, 18
  elaborating, 68–69
  generative, 65–78
  gradebooks in, 100, 103, 109–111
  identity formation and, 17
  misperceptions about, 18, 20
  passive, 65
  personalizing, 68–69
  process of, 69–70
  progressions, 24, 31–34
  reporting structures on, 109–118
  respect for, 19
  responsibility for, 79
  rubrics in, 49, 52
  scrutinizing, 68–69
  self-deliberation and, 91–92
  self-reliant, 18, 19
  teaching with student vs. teaching thinking, 67, 75
  transactional vs. generative, 12, 13
  transient, guarding against, 18, 19
  what it looks like, 12
learning gaps, 83
learning stories, 109
lesson planning, instructional diamond for, 67–69, 73–75
Lewis, J. L., 17
life satisfaction, 8, 18
logic rule, 101, 107

M

mastery experiences, 20, 62, 67–69, 76, 82
mathematics
  assumption-proof assessment in, 60
  co-constructed feedback on, 82–83
  proficiency scales for, 27
  rubrics for, 47
McDaniel, M. A., 70
McGivney, E., 23
Melbourne Education Research Institute, 18
mental models, 59–61
mentors and mentoring, 18, 19
metacognition, 91, 97
misperceptions about learning, 18, 20
missing work, 113
mission statements, 7
  academic acuity and interest in, 16
  aligning, 120
  characteristics of student-centered, 16–21
  creating student-centered, 15–22
  culture and, 21
  developing, 18–21

guarding against transient learning in, 18, 19
misperceptions about learning and, 18, 20
recommendations for implementing, 21–22
sample, 21
self-reliant learning valued in, 18, 19
social connection in, 16–17
student-produced evidence and, 18, 20
motivation
emotional awareness, self-concept, and, 17
self-efficacy and, 8, 9
Mount Vernon High School, Mount Vernon, Iowa, 1–2, 117, 119–122
feedback at, 83
grading at, 101
mission statement, 16
reflection at, 95
music, rubrics for, 45

N

Next Generation Science Standards, 24
nonevaluative language, 80, 84–85
nonrecursive criteria, 36

O

Osborne, J. W., 16

P

parents, communicating with, 105
passive learning, 65
pausing evaluation, 85
pedagogical practices, 14
inseparability of assessment and instruction, 71–73
instructional diamond, 67–69, 73–75
mastery experiences, 67–69
success criteria and, 36
personal efficacy, 8
physical engagement, 89–90
political science, rubrics for, 48
practice of failing, 70. *See also* failure
preparation, reporting on student, 111, 114–116
prescriptive feedback, 80–81
process-based assessments, 56–61
proficiency, lasting vs. transient, 67
proficiency gradations, 24, 26–28
aligning with letter grades, 100, 101–102
creating effective, 33
generative learning and, 76
learning progressions vs., 24, 31–34
logic rule for, 101, 107
reperformances and, 100, 102–103
rubrics and, 44–48
setting criteria for, 24, 28–31
using during instruction, 67, 70
purpose, reflection on, 92

Q

questions, serious self-questioning and reflection, 91

R

recursive criteria, 35
reflection and introspection, 89–97
accurate perception of abilities and, 10–11
differentiated, 91, 93–95
gradebooks in, 100, 103
on growth, 93
how to add to lessons, 90–95
learning after, 89
pausing evaluation for, 85
personal, 93
reliable reflective mechanics for, 91, 92–93
reperformance and, 95–96, 97
rubrics and, 44–48
self-deliberation and, 91–92
serious self-questioning in, 91
simulations for, 59
remediation, 9
reperformance, 95–96, 97
grading and, 100, 102–103
reporting structures, 109–118
characteristics of dynamic, 109–116
recommendations for implementing, 117
on student behavior, 111, 113–114
on student growth, 111, 112
on student performance, 111, 112–113
on student preparation, 111, 114–116
respect, for learning, 19–20
Rettig, M., 17
Rinkema, E., 34
Roediger, H. L., 70
rubrics, student-centered, 43–54
for conversation, 49–51
for feedback, 49, 51–52
generative learning and, 76
how to create, 44–48
how to use, 49–52
in the learning process, 49, 52
positive language in, 80, 83
prescriptive vs. diagnostic, 80–81
traditional rubrics vs., 49–52

S

scaffolding, 71
scales, proficiency, 24, 26–28
Schimmer, T., 79
Schoemaker, P. J. H., 89
science skills
  criteria for proficiency gradations, 29–30
  instructional diamond for lesson planning, 74
  proficiency scales for, 27
  rubrics for, 46
  success criteria for, 35
self-appraisal, 10–11
  differentiated reflection and, 91, 93–95
  rubrics and, 43, 44, 49–53
  simulations for, 59
self-awareness, 59
self-concept, positive, 8, 9, 16, 17
self-deliberation, 91–92
self-efficacy, 7–8
  assessments and, 61
  definition of, 17–18
  mission statements and, 16, 17–18
  proficiency gradations and, 34
  rubrics and, 44
  well-being and, 8
self-regulation, 10–11
self-reliance, 8, 75
  mission statements and, 22
  valued in mission statements, 18, 19
self-sufficiency, 20
self-sustenance, 8, 9
shadows, cast, 32
simulations, 57, 59, 61
  summative, 81
skills
  arranging assessments by, 58
  creating standards for, 24, 25–26
  curriculum organization around, 23–41
  developing proficiency gradations for, 24, 26–28
  enduring, transferable, 24–25, 36
  recursive vs. nonrecursive criteria and, 24, 34–36
  reflection on, 92
social connection, 8, 11, 16–17
social studies skills
  criteria for proficiency gradations, 29–30
  proficiency gradations for, 28, 33
social-emotional development, 18, 58
  reporting on, 111, 113–114
Stalets, M., 79
standards
  arranging assessments by, 58, 61
  assessment development and, 57
  creating for skills, 24, 25–26
  defining, 57
  developing proficiency gradations for, 24, 26–28
  shadows with, 32
  skills-based curriculum and, 24
stereotypes, 17
Stevenson. *See* Adlai E. Stevenson High School, Illinois
student preparation, reporting on, 111, 114–116
student-does-first instructional model, 75
success
  communication and, 8, 11
  guidelines for redefining, 8–11
  perception of abilities and, 8, 10–11
  positive self-concept and, 8, 9
  recursive vs. nonrecursive criteria for, 24, 34–36
  redefining student, 7–14
  self-sustenance and, 8, 9
  setting criteria for proficiency gradations and, 24, 28–31
  social connection, emotional awareness, and, 8, 11
success criteria, 34–36, 43. *See also* rubrics, student-centered
  arranging assessments by, 58
  co-constructed feedback with, 82–83
  reflection on, 92
  rubrics and, 44–48
summative experiences, 80, 81

T

teachers, social connection with, 17
tetherball metaphor of feedback, 80
transactional learning, 12

V

Vagle, N. D., 43
values, connecting learning with, 9

W

Wagner, T., 7, 15
White, K., 89
Williams, S., 34
Winthrop, R., 23
Wood, R. E., 8
Woolfolk Hoy, A., 18
work, missing, 100, 104–105, 113

Z

Zimmermann, B. J., 17–18

Proficiency-Based Instruction
Eric Twadell, Mark Onuscheck, Anthony R. Reibel, and Troy Gobble
Only by shifting away from a one-size-fits-all approach to teaching and learning can every student achieve true success in the classroom. In this resource, the authors share a clear five-step process for educators to seamlessly transition to proficiency-based instruction.
BKF838

Proficiency-Based Assessment
Troy Gobble, Mark Onuscheck, Anthony R. Reibel, and Eric Twadell
With this resource, teachers will discover how to close the gaps between assessment, curriculum, and instruction by replacing outmoded assessment methods with proficiency-based assessments. Learn the essentials of proficiency-based assessment, and explore evidence-based strategies for successful implementation.
BKF631

Pathways to Proficiency
Troy Gobble, Mark Onuscheck, Anthony R. Reibel, and Eric Twadell
Adopt a new, more effective grading model for students. This book provides the pathway for implementing evidence-based grading practices in schools through a straightforward, five-phase creative model. Readers will follow a hypothetical curriculum team's challenging journey through each phase of this process.
BKF682

Proficiency-Based Grading in the Content Areas
Edited by Anthony R. Reibel and Eric Twadell
No matter the content area, evidence-based grading puts student growth at the heart of the classroom. Designed for teachers and administrators of grades 6–12, *Proficiency-Based Grading in the Content Areas* details how to effectively implement evidence-based grading and maintain its effectiveness over time.
BKF837

Solution Tree | Press

Visit SolutionTree.com or call 800.733.6786 to order.

"Excellent engagement in what truly matters in **assessment**.

Great examples!"

—Carol Johnson, superintendent,
Central Dauphin School District, Pennsylvania

 PD Services

Our experts draw from decades of research and their own experiences to bring you practical strategies for designing and implementing quality assessments. You can choose from a range of customizable services, from a one-day overview to a multiyear process.

Book your assessment PD today!
888.763.9045

Solution Tree